PRAISE FOR
BUSINESS IS ART

"A clear winner in terms of finding solutions to help achieve your long- and short-term business goals."

DR. SANJAY JAIN, *NEW YORK TIMES* BESTSELLING AUTHOR OF *OPTIMAL LIVING 360*

"*Business Is ART* will help anyone who is starting out or needs to refresh their skills in this highly competitive business environment. Jon breaks down the fundamentals in a way that is both fun to read and thought provoking. Anyone looking for new thoughts about how to succeed should be reading this."

KIM KELLY-BARTLEY, VICE PRESIDENT, MARKETING AND MENU DEVELOPMENT, WHITE CASTLE MANAGEMENT CO.

"An excellent resource for start-ups, existing businesses, and companies wanting to retool themselves. Jon is an amazing guide—you will keep returning to his words over and again!"

PAUL BUTARE, FORMER CEO, ACROSOFT CORPORATION

"Success doesn't happen to you. You create success. In *Business Is ART*, Jon Umstead uses his own experiences to guide you along the envisioning, tracking, and attainment of your short- and long-term goals. A great tool no matter where you are in your life or career."

MICHAEL MCDORMAN, PRESIDENT & CEO, GREATER SPRINGFIELD CHAMBER OF COMMERCE

"I provided coaching services to Jon during the growth period used as a case study in *Business Is ART*. He captures the experience well and provides great examples and tools that business owners and organizational leaders can use to create higher levels of success."

RICH TAFEL, PRESIDENT, PUBLIC SQUARED

BUSINESS

IS

ART*

*and science, gut instinct, hard work,
and a certain amount of luck*

JON UMSTEAD

Figure.1
Vancouver / Berkeley

Cataloguing data available from Library and Archives Canada
ISBN 978-1-927958-44-5 (pbk.)
ISBN 978-1-927958-55-1 (hbk.)
ISBN 978-1-927958-45-2 (ebook)
ISBN 978-1-927958-47-6 (pdf)

Editing by Michael Schellenberg
Copy editing by Eva van Emden
Index by François Trahan
Design by Ingrid Paulson
Printed and bound in Canada by Friesens
Distributed in the U.S. by Publishers Group West

Figure 1 Publishing Inc.
Vancouver BC Canada
www.figure1pub.com

CONTENTS

ix   **FOREWORD**

1   **INTRODUCTION | BUSINESS IS ART**

5   **ONE | BUSINESS IS ART**
6   Twelve Steps to Business as ART
8   Start with a Vision
11   Self-Assessment
23   Paint the Picture
28   Dream Big but Have Some Basis in Reality
30   Now Comes Strategy
31   A Note on Vision, Mission, and Purpose
32   The Chapter 1 Wrap

34   **TWO | REFUSING TO BE CONSTRAINED BY THE SHACKLES OF CHOREOGRAPHY**
38   Dancing Elephants
41   Radical Change
43   No Shackles with No Plan Is a Waste of Time
46   The Shackles Are Developing Faster and Faster

47 Staying Relevant

50 Implore to Explore

52 The Chapter 2 Wrap

54 THREE | STRATEGIC PLANNING

60 Common Myths about Strategic Planning

66 Revise or Refine the Vision as Necessary

69 Honestly Assess Today's Situation

70 Recognize the Gaps and Identify the Goals and Objectives

71 Identify Strategic Initiatives

73 Common Elements of a Strategic Plan

75 The ProCESS Strategy

76 The One-Page Strategic Plan

78 The Chapter 3 Wrap

80 FOUR | STRATEGIC MANAGEMENT

81 Dust: The Difference between Strategic
   Planning and Strategic Management

82 Task Management versus Strategic Management

84 Determine How You Will Manage Strategic Initiatives

87 The Basic Components of a Project Plan

90 A Word on Delegating

93 Strategic Management of Customers

96 Avoid the Big Lie

99 The Chapter 4 Wrap

101 FIVE | BEHAVIOR MANAGEMENT

103 Behavior Management Starts with You

106 After You, Behavior Management Starts
    with Common Courtesy

110 The Three Pillars of Behavior Management

112   The Three Pillars Defined
120   Behavior Management Myths
131   Bonus and Pay-for-Performance Plans
140   The Chapter 5 Wrap

142   **SIX | THE BUSINESS PLAN**
143   Why Would You Not Have a Business Plan?
144   The Business Is ART Business Plan Template
165   I Have a Plan—Now What?
167   Well, *That* Didn't Work!
169   Prepare Yourself for Tough Choices
175   The Chapter 6 Wrap

177   **SEVEN | THE IMPORTANCE OF METRICS**
180   Tracking Performance Is a Discipline
181   Key Performance Indicators
187   Don't Track Everything
190   Don't Be Afraid to Think Big
191   The Chapter 7 Wrap

193   **EIGHT | CORRELATING METRICS**
195   Cause and Effect
197   Pairing Theory
200   KPI Pairing Recommendations
216   The Chapter 8 Wrap

218   **NINE | PING CHARTING**
220   Pictures and Graphs and Charts, Oh My!
222   The Origins of the Ping Chart
223   Foundations of the Ping Chart

227 Plotting the Ping Chart
232 Interpreting the Ping Chart
235 The Pursuit of Trivia
236 But I Already Did My Plan!
237 A Word on Resistance to Change
245 The Chapter 9 Wrap

248 TEN | THE BUSINESS IS ART WRAP
255 The Business Is ART Software
256 A Final Word

259 INDEX

FOREWORD

As one of the faculty of Jon's Executive MBA program, I knew that he had a lot to say and that he would make the most of his experience. *Business Is ART* is an inspiring collection of the best of a professional business school education, tempered with insight, humor, and the wisdom that comes from years of practical experience.

Not everyone has the means, desire, or need to seek an advanced degree in business, but every business owner and organizational leader needs to understand and apply the basic principles of good business practices. From business novices looking for tools to help them get to the next level to seasoned professionals looking for refresher material, readers from all parts of the business world will find their odds of success improved when they apply the basic principles provided by *Business Is ART*.

And who doesn't want better odds?

Roy Lewicki, Irving Abramowitz Memorial Professor Emeritus,
The Ohio State University Fisher College of Business

INTRODUCTION

BUSINESS IS ART

*Being good in business is the most fascinating
kind of art. Making money is art and
working is art and good business is the best art.*

ANDY WARHOL

There are some who would argue that business is a science. My undergraduate degree is in fact a bachelor of science in management science. That's a lot of science for a guy who has never owned a lab coat. While I believe there are scientific approaches, disciplines, and principles that one should apply to business in order to be more effective at it, I also believe that there is at least an equal, if not greater, part to business success that is art.

And so, I subscribe to a combination of theories. There is a science to business, but business is art (as well as gut instinct, hard work, and a certain amount of luck). This book plays to both sides of this theory, at times discussing the science of business, and at times the artful nature of it. But I want to emphasize the artful side of the process. In so doing, I have developed an acronym—because no business book worth its salt would be complete without one—that reflects both sides of the theory: ART.

A = Articulate
R = Revise
T = Track

Business Is ART. To be as effective as you can be, you must *articulate* what it is you want, *revise* your plans as you go along, and *track* your results so that you know what needs to be revised and how, and so that you can better articulate what it is you want. Do you see the cycle here?

Do this at every level of planning and for every type of plan, be it a strategic plan, a project plan, or a simple task list. There is great power in writing down what it is you want, being flexible enough to change your approach as needed, and formally observing your progress. Follow this simple ARTful approach and you will be amazed at how much you are able to achieve.

Only he is an emancipated thinker who is not afraid to write foolish things.
ANTON CHEKHOV, RUSSIAN PHYSICIAN AND AUTHOR

Business can be a complex portrait made up of many shapes, faces, figures, scenes, colors, and hues. It is our job as the ARTists to bring all of these components together to create our own masterpieces. It requires the creativity, imagination, and intuition of an artist. The best artist knows that rigor is key to success and that successful creation requires the methodical approach of a scientist.

This book discusses some of the primary components of a business "masterpiece," including strategic planning, strategic management, and the importance of metrics. Metrics may also be referred to as key performance indicators, objectives, targets, or any number of other terms. Simply put, they represent the measurements you keep to track how you are doing.

The book also introduces a new way to visualize, think about, and track metrics that may help you picture and then create your own work of ART: "Ping Charting." A "Ping Chart" helps you visualize and analyze correlation, or the cause and effect metrics have on one another, by viewing metrics in pairs rather than as singular items, providing you with a more complete picture of performance. As you will learn, it combines the 4.0 grading system that is common in the United States with the visual pings that you see on a sonar screen.

Now I know what you're thinking: "Oh goody! Metrics! And new ways to track them! Sure, I'll read this book right after I finish jabbing this hot iron rod into my eye, because in the grand scheme of things, and by order of preference, having a hot iron rod jabbed into my eye comes before talking about metrics."

But before you stoke that fire, let me assure you that I have tried to make this book both informative and entertaining. It is my great hope that it will make you laugh, think, and learn, because like you, I don't want to read one more business book that makes me feel like I'd rather be heating up that iron rod.

Most importantly, it is my great hope that this book will actually inspire you to *do something with what you have learned*. Business Is ART. Articulate. Revise. Track. Rinse and repeat.

ONE

BUSINESS IS ART

Don't bury your thoughts; put your vision to reality.

BOB MARLEY

As mentioned in the introduction, I believe that business is a combination of science and art. We apply learned theory, methods, and practices to business (science). But any business must first begin with a vision: an idea (art). The business is an act of creation by its maker (the artist), but a large number of business failures happen because the artist doesn't apply business practice (science).

An excellent baker opens a bakery that fails because it is not run as a business. They may focus on the yeast, sugars, and recipes required to produce the most delicious bread in town, but may fail to track and estimate the costs of ingredients and the labor and overhead that go into production, resulting in a pricing model that makes no business sense. They may ignore potential foot traffic into the shop, or run an ineffective marketing campaign, not necessarily because the skills to do so are absent, but because the focus is always on the baked good itself.

The "starving artist" theory would apply here, were it not for the shelves full of delicious artisan bread that no one is buying, and therefore, the artist can use to feed the family. But after a couple of days, it grows stale and moldy. Personally, sometimes I like the extra crunch of day-old, stale bread. But mold? Yuck.

On the other hand, far too often business owners and leaders forget, or never realize, that they necessarily created (and must nurture) the business as an artist. All too quickly they move into practitioner mode (scientist). This is when the business can lose its soul. Gasp.

The successful business leader is both scientist and artist. *Business Is ART* is designed to keep those two roles in lockstep with one another.

■ TWELVE STEPS TO BUSINESS AS ART

While ART is a simple acronym and concept, there are many crucial details lying underneath.

A business begins with the vision. If you can envision it, then the next step is to articulate it. You must articulate it to make it real. But where does this vision come from?

Thomas Edison famously said, "Genius is one percent inspiration and ninety-nine percent perspiration," and the same may be true for inspiration itself for some people.

For the more fortunate souls, the ability to create a vision is almost mystical or otherworldly. The vision just appears in their minds. Some people wake up dreaming about something that becomes their vision. But others really have to think it through—to think about their situation and what it is that they want in a more deliberate way—before they can develop a vision.

Regardless, in all cases, it starts with an idea that needs to be explored. This exploration can take on many forms. This book provides you with just one means to conduct that exploration; it's one possible process out of many that may work for you as it has for me.

You will find details, examples, and backstories that support the process of taking that vision and making it a reality within the book; however, here is the twelve-step process, or science, to approach business as an ART. Each step is illustrated later:

1. Briefly articulate the vision.
2. Conduct a self-assessment that includes your own personal definition of success.
3. Paint the picture by creating a document of at most three pages, or better yet, an actual work of art such as a painting, a video, or a web site that visually tells your story.
4. Revise or refine the vision if necessary.
5. Honestly assess today's reality versus tomorrow's vision.
6. Recognize the gaps between the vision and today's reality.

7. Identify goals that you will have to meet in order to close the gap, and define objectives that will measure the rate of success in achieving those goals.
8. Identify specific initiatives, projects, or actions that have to be taken to realize those objectives.
9. Determine how you will manage the initiatives (project planning) and measure progress toward the completion of those initiatives.
10. Determine how you will manage the business itself.
11. Execute the plans and regularly measure your progress.
12. Continue to review, assess, refine, and modify the previous steps as necessary.

As you will note, this twelve-step process involves a healthy mix of science and art. Creating the vision, determining goals and objectives, and identifying initiatives or actions necessary to achieve them fall into the realm of art more than science. These tasks require imagination. On the more scientific side are developing detailed project plans, executing them, and measuring progress.

Let's start with the vision.

■ START WITH A VISION

Throughout this book we use a real example of a time when I very successfully followed this twelve-step method. I had been assigned to lead an acquired company that had 170 employees, an annual revenue of just over $21 million, and a net profit a bit under 10 percent. This was an information technology company that did a little bit of business process outsourcing on the side. It had existed for more than twenty-five years. Until my assignment, the founders were still there leading the company. Many employees had never been employed by anyone else, and nepotism was not a dirty word.

I didn't know much about the particular markets in which the company was involved, but I knew about organizational leadership, people, and the business of business. Initially, my only vision for this company was to just not screw it up. After all, we had acquired it because there was perceived value in it. I knew I would want to do more with it than that eventually, but initially, that was it: just don't screw it up. What I really wanted to do was to get in there and grow this company. Thankfully, I was just barely smart enough to realize that I had to look before leaping. Being unfamiliar with the business, there were a few things I needed to do before making any big moves.

So, my first order of business was to learn more about the markets, the services, and the products in order to get to the bottom of how my vision for the company would establish itself. I took time to get to know the people and the culture of the company. I used a disciplined approach, and the time I spent doing this was invaluable. I met with my direct staff and employees frequently, talked to customers, reviewed contracts and proposals, and did a little market research. I also employed consultants as subject matter experts when it made sense to do so.

Fortunately, I was allowed to take my time, which is not always the case. Sometimes the pressure is too great, or the need to turn things around too urgent. As I became more knowledgeable about the business, I began to formulate thoughts and envision the future. It was a great place to be because I wasn't starting from a blank canvas. In this case, I had quite a lot to start with.

As I mentioned, this had been a successful company, in business for more than twenty-five years when I took it over. It was profitable. It had recurring and predictable revenue. It had a great culture, but it lacked growth and opportunity, and the margins were just barely acceptable. While it was an enjoyable place for its employees to work, as a business it had become stagnant. If things didn't change soon, the business would begin to decline. In fact, we had already lost significant ground in two markets where we had once been the clear leader.

After going through all of this learning and assessment, I thought this company could relatively easily double in size, and maybe go a little further than that if we looked at things a little differently and took a few calculated risks. I began to envision a $50 million company that would lead a couple of niche markets in business process outsourcing services enabled by exceptional technology, as opposed to an information technology company that dabbled in outsourcing services. My vision began to emerge: step one. Now for step two.

■ SELF-ASSESSMENT

> *Perhaps the best place to begin with an integral*
> *approach to business is with oneself. In the Big Three*
> *of self, culture, and world, integral mastery starts with*
> *self. How do body, mind, and spirit operate in me?*
> *How does that necessarily impact my role in the world*
> *of business? And how can I become more conscious of*
> *these already operating realities in myself and in others?*
>
> KEN WILBER, AMERICAN AUTHOR,
>
> *A BRIEF HISTORY OF EVERYTHING*

Step two is a self-assessment. You may be wondering why self-assessment would be included as an early and important part of a twelve-step process to approaching business as an ART.

Before you go too far in creating your vision, I encourage all of you, regardless of your position in the company, to go through a self-assessment process. If at all possible, use a professional coach or a peer group: these are unbiased people with no skin in the game other than to help you succeed, people who are willing to listen to you and will respectfully shoot straight with you. Bartenders and your old dog don't count.

Through this process, define what success means to you and how you will achieve it. This is vitally important because if your personal mission and definition of success do not align with your company/professional vision, then your life will be out of balance, and you will have to make some changes to bring it back. When this misalignment occurs, you will go through a range of questions and emotions, rarely good ones, on a regular basis.

The song "Once in a Lifetime" by the band Talking Heads does exactly that. The main character portrayed in the song reaches a point in life where he questions everything he owns and has accomplished. He has focused so much on those things that he has missed everything that is important in life.

When your personal vision and mission do not align with your professional vision and mission, you will sadly miss many of those once-in-a-lifetime moments. *Same as it ever was.*

But let's use some wisdom. The "how to succeed" business is a multibillion dollar industry. It's not hard to find any number of gurus out there who will tell you how to succeed at whatever you endeavor, whether it is to become wealthy, lose thirty pounds, or become a writer, model, actor, or artist—you name it. But is there really an answer to the question of how to succeed?

Before coming to that, it's important to first answer this question for yourself: "How do I define success?"

What is important to you? Is success a high-paying career? Is it to own your own business? Is it to be the perfect parent, spouse, or friend? Perhaps your definition of success is to learn to cook meals three times a week for your family. It is not so important how you define success, but it is critical that you do.

My own life and career have been filled with twists, turns, bumps, grinds, victories, and defeats. In general, I always had a vision of where I wanted to be in life, but I relied on my education, instincts, and dumb luck to get there. It was only a few years ago that I formally developed a plan. I looked at my past successes and failures and used them to help me determine what I could accomplish next. With the assistance of a coach, I considered the following four major categories in setting out my plan:

1. Current job
2. Career
3. Family (By any definition, including friends and pets.)
4. Spirituality (This is often not addressed in the professional coaching world. I am not using it here to mean "religion," although it certainly can be. I am using it as a catchall for those things that make you a "better person.")

Classic coaching techniques focus on the first three items in this list, and sometimes throw in spirituality (I recommend including this). Consider these three or four categories simultaneously to optimize your work-life balance. Critics say there is no such thing, but even if that's true, it is important to strive for it.

The scales may always tip one way or another, with one side or the other weighing more heavily at any given point in time. But if the scales are static, with one side constantly weighted more heavily than the other, you have problems.

The next section provides a template that you can use for your self-assessment.

■ SELF-ASSESSMENT TEMPLATE

- Envision the future. What is your definition of success?
- What is your personal mission or purpose?
- What are your blind spots (things that can hinder your success, perhaps things you do not yet recognize in yourself)?
- What are your strengths?
- What are your objectives?

TABLE 1.1. SELF-ASSESSMENT WORKSHEET: OBJECTIVES.

CATEGORY	SHORT-TERM OBJECTIVES (NEXT 6 MONTHS)	MEDIUM-TERM OBJECTIVES	LONG-TERM OBJECTIVES (3 YEARS AND BEYOND)
Current Job	1.	1.	1.
	2.	2.	2.
	3.	3.	3.
Career	1.	1.	1.
	2.	2.	2.
	3.	3.	3.
Family	1.	1.	1.
	2.	2.	2.
	3.	3.	3.
Spiritual (Optional)	1.	1.	1.
	2.	2.	2.
	3.	3.	3.

· What do you need to do to achieve your objectives (personal action items)?

TABLE 1.2. SELF-ASSESSMENT WORKSHEET: ACTIONS NEEDED TO ACHIEVE YOUR OBJECTIVES.

ACTION	OBJECTIVE(S) SERVED	DUE DATE

Modify and review this template with your coach on a regular, perhaps monthly, basis. Don't try to complete it all in one sitting. Do one step at a time and then review with your coach. Before moving forward, review everything you already did. Does everything still make sense? Is everything on target? Make sure you are satisfied with everything before going to the next step.

This is especially beneficial when considering your strengths and your objectives. Many coaching techniques will tell you to focus on improving your weaknesses, but I believe it's better to play to your strengths. Be aware of your blind spots, but play to your strengths. Your strengths are what will carry you through.

For example, it is perfectly fine to say, "You know, I'm not really good at math and I want to be."

Then do something about it. Get better at it. Heck, make it a strength if that is what you want or need to succeed. But as you do, play to your strengths. Maybe you are really great socially. If so, don't try to improve your math skills on your own. Join a class and form a study group. With the study group, you are playing to your strength as a social extrovert.

Now comes the tough part. Follow through. Do the things you need to do to achieve your objectives. Measure your progress regularly. Don't do it any less frequently than monthly. As you do, you will find one of several things becomes clear:

- You were right on target with everything defined in the six steps.
- What you thought was important to you now seems less so (if you aren't making time to meet your objective, then it must not be as important to you as you thought).
- Your priorities are all wrong.

But the most important thing you will find is that you will achieve your objectives with astounding speed. It never ceases to amaze me how achievable something is when I commit it to paper and repeatedly say it out loud.

For example, when I went through this process with my coach for the very first time, it became clear to me that I was much more passionate about social politics and business than I had realized, or had been up to that point. The realization put me at a crossroads. As I identified my personal objectives, I realized that I wanted to run for an elected office or get an MBA, but there was not time for both.

I wrote both goals down in my self-assessment and reviewed them regularly with my coach. In less than six months, I found myself throwing my hat into the ring to run for a state representative position that suddenly opened up. One short month later, I realized I was not cut out for politics and focused instead on an MBA. Eighteen months after that, I graduated. None of that would have happened had I not laid it out on paper.

As you go through this process, you will undoubtedly discover things about yourself and about the people who mean the most to you. You will find yourself adjusting vision, mission, objectives, etc., accordingly. You may even find it is time to take a huge leap of faith. If so, it is wise to be scared, but it is foolish to let that fear paralyze you.

In his autobiography, Nelson Mandela says, "The brave man is not he who does not feel afraid, but he who conquers that fear." Words to live by.

Now back to my own experience. Around the time that I was beginning to formulate a vision for the company, I hired a life coach. As discussed, with the assistance of my coach we did a detailed personal assessment of me as an individual. My experience with my life coach helped me realize that I was indeed in the right job at the right time and that the vision I was beginning to formulate for the company was in line with who I was and who I wanted to be. Without that alignment, it is doubtful that the company would ultimately have been as successful as it was.

Sometimes, it just takes a leap of faith.

During my first job out of college, I worked with a retired military paramedic who had actually had to jump from a helicopter to find a seriously injured fighter pilot.

He then hid with the pilot and cared for him in the jungles of Vietnam for three days. Talk about being scared. Talk about a leap of faith.

This guy's name was Larry and he always used to say, "If at first you don't succeed, keep on sucking 'til you do succeed."

I was twenty-three, and he used to say it a lot, so it really irritated me at the time. But years later, I came to appreciate what Larry was trying to say. When you feel afraid or unsure, or you fail or make missteps—and you will—don't beat yourself up over it, don't let it paralyze you, and don't point fingers. Simply jump, learn from what went well and what didn't, then apply the lessons learned to the next jump. But don't give up, and don't let fear of failure stop you.

I've missed more than 9,000 shots in my career. I've lost almost 300 games. Twenty-six times, I've been entrusted to take the game winning shot and missed. I've failed over and over and over again in my life. And that is why I succeed.

MICHAEL JORDAN

Note: he probably didn't say that so eloquently on the first attempt!

So what is the secret to success? As you might expect, there is no silver bullet. Success doesn't happen to you. You create success. Anything you create can be considered art; always remember ART as an acronym for "articulate," "refine," and "track."

If you *articulate* what success means to you and how you will achieve it, *refine* both your definition of success and your steps along the way, and *track* your progress, you will succeed in the vast majority of your endeavors, in much shorter time frames than you had imagined, no matter how you define success. And I'll emphasize it again: tracking is so vitally important and so often ignored.

A final note on your self-assessment: I completed my Executive MBA at the Ohio State University (it's a rule to put "the" in front of "Ohio State University" or else the Buckeye Police take your diploma in the middle of the night). For one of our courses, we were challenged to write and present, in less than five minutes, our individual "leadership legacy statement."

On the day of our presentations, one by one, each of the fifty members of our cohort stood up and presented their leadership legacy statement. We were often moved to tears, we frequently laughed, and we were truly inspired by one another. Several of us commented after the fact that we wished we had completed this exercise much earlier in the program because as a result of it, we felt we knew one another on a much deeper level. Our appreciation for one another had grown immensely.

It was an excellent exercise in self-assessment, and I recommend that everyone give it a shot. I felt so moved by the experience that I brought it back to the organization I ran at the time and asked each and every one of our managers to go through it. As they each presented their statements, I took notes. In reviewing the notes, common themes appeared. I took those common themes and drafted up a group leadership legacy statement that everyone signed off on. We framed it and put it on the wall.

It was one of the best things we ever did to get to know each other on a more personal level and communicate how we really wanted to be viewed by our employees. See the sidebar below for a detailed view of our group leadership legacy statement.

OUR LEADERSHIP LEGACY STATEMENT

As a leader, it is my responsibility to own and communicate a vision for those who would follow. It is then my responsibility to make sure a plan to get there is created and managed. These are my responsibilities, but my leadership legacy is something more.

As a leader, my actions speak louder than my words. I need to be visible so that others can see me give of myself, hold myself accountable, and move in a decisive manner so that they, in turn, will be driven to strive for greatness. After all, it is greatness that I want for them. Throughout our journey, they must know that they can approach me with good news and bad, and that I expect them to come to the table with solutions, not complaints, as I will. I act with a sense of humility, recognizing and appreciating the efforts and achievements of others.

As a leader, I am empathetic to others. I recognize that I am engaging with real people, not positions. I am engaging with real people, not email or mailing addresses. I am engaging with real people, not voices on the phone. I am engaging with real people who have real lives outside of work, and I must ensure that they are properly balancing work and life. I must truly listen to what they are saying and feeling, not necessarily to the words they use. To do so sometimes requires my patience and always, my caring.

As a leader, I instill trust. Sometimes trust comes without condition. Sometimes, trust must be earned. At all times, trust must be nurtured. Trust does not come without honesty and respect. I must protect an environment of equality, fairness, and inclusion in order for trust to flourish.

As a leader, I teach others. Communication is the framework of teaching. I must be willing to share what I know and what I believe when appropriate. Others may not necessarily agree with what I have to say, but I must at least say it and then provide my reasoning, so that others may form their own thoughts and opinions, learning from my knowledge and experience, even if that means ultimately moving in another direction.

As a leader, I am flexible. The circumstances around me will always change, usually outside of my control. I therefore continually embrace change and adapt. Sometimes change does not come without risk. I must be smart enough to recognize the risk, brave enough to accept it, and creative enough to mitigate it.

As a leader, I never stop learning. Likewise, I never stop encouraging others to learn. Learning is not limited to reading the success stories of others, earning a degree or certification or completing a class. These are all important components to learning. But I must also learn from my mistakes. I must create an environment in which it is acceptable for others to make mistakes, to learn from those mistakes, and look ahead to continuous improvement, not back to find points of blame.

As a leader, I contribute to the growth of others. Others grow when they are prepared, encouraged, and permitted to take on new growth opportunities. It is my responsibility to make sure that growth opportunities are created and communicated. Whether a person seeks opportunities within or outside of my area of responsibility, I do not discourage them nor stand in the way. I challenge people to grow and let them know they are expected to enable the growth of others.

As a leader, I recognize the strengths of others. In order to do so, I must first understand and know myself well. I have my own strengths, but I am not infallible. I have weaknesses. I must use my strengths, but I must recognize and use the strengths of others and my team to succeed.

As a leader, I create and promote teamwork. I motivate and inspire my team to do great things. I am the keeper of team morale. It is important to work hard, but to also have fun and enjoy what we do.

As a leader, I celebrate our success. Success does not always have to be measured in large numbers. It is as important to celebrate the little things as it is the big.

■ PAINT THE PICTURE

In his book *Double Double*, Cameron Herold provides advice on how to double your revenue and profit in three years.

His book discusses the importance and value of visualizing the organization and the future in what he refers to as the "painted picture." To avoid confusion, let me describe what he means by this. It should be a written document of roughly three pages that describes "in vivid detail" what the company (or organization) "will look and feel like three years out." It describes the importance of initially focusing on what you want, as opposed to how you get there. The painted picture differs from the vision statement in that the vision is a component of the painted picture. The vision is a quick statement, while the painted picture goes into more detail.

The painted picture allows you to tell your story so that employees, investors, clients, analysts, and anyone else listening and watching can picture at a glance *exactly* what this beast will be. It doesn't matter what it is right now. It doesn't matter how many obstacles and hurdles stand in the way. It doesn't matter how you plan to get there: that comes later. What matters up front is the painted picture, because without it, no path forward can be derived.

Imagine you are getting ready to take a vacation. All romantic notions of jumping in the car and seeing where the road takes you aside, most of us travel with the explicit objective of getting to a specific place. We start with the end—the destination—in mind. Determining how (or if) we are going to get there comes later. Determining where we are going comes first.

It is the same in business and is Herold's (and my) point exactly. Paint the picture without worrying about how you will make it come true. The notion of painting the picture fits very nicely within the Business Is ART framework, and so I have included it as step three in the twelve-step process. Indeed, this is one step we unwittingly completed in our quest to grow to $50 million, which will be explained later.

Herold suggests you pretend that you have traveled forward in time and are walking around the company with a clipboard in hand, going through a checklist that assesses every aspect of the business. He even provides a list of sample questions to ask, such as, What are you seeing and hearing? What are others saying about your business? You may want to add more questions to your list, such as, How do you give back to the community? How do employees see their career paths? What is their average tenure?

I encourage you to literally turn your painted picture into a work of art. Create a web page, produce a video, write a song, create a visual representation that you hang on the wall. Do something beyond a text-based document. Truly, and in the literal sense, make the painted picture artful.

My vision for the company was to see it at least double in size and to be focused on the delivery of business process services enabled by great technology, as opposed to being a great technology service provider that also delivered some business processes.

This company was disjointed and operating like four separate companies, except on potluck lunch days, in which case it was one big happy and well-fed family. But there was a common thread that would help us establish more of a "one company" environment: about 95 percent of our revenue originated from the federal government. The company had made a name for itself in some niche markets and services in which federally funded programs were delivered either at the state level or directly by the private sector. These states and private sector businesses were our clients.

Further, the states could not deliver the end service except in partnership with the private sector. Programs like this are called public–private partnerships, or P3s. The company had prospered in P3 business but was just kind of flopping around whenever it tried to sell services and solutions exclusively to the private sector.

Consequently, I felt we should stop flopping around and focus our attention solely on P3. The details are not important here, but what is important is that an initial vision began to emerge, and through the initial vision phase, the canvas for a painted picture was established. But it needed a lot more work.

This company was not integrated in any fashion beyond human resources and payroll. As mentioned before, it was really a collection of four smaller companies, each serving a different market. Each subunit had its own set of products, services, processes, leaders, and sales and marketing campaigns. In many cases, functions overlapped or were redundant. So in addition to there being no common vision for moving the organization as a whole forward, there was also a lot of inefficiency and unnecessary costs.

It was easy for me as a newcomer and relative outsider to see how disjointed the company was, but it was very difficult for the employees and management team to see it, because to them it was the status quo and it was how they had grown with the company. But although this method of doing business had served well for many years, it had maxed out its potential.

Sometimes that's all it takes: just one fresh set of eyes to look at something and see it differently than everyone else who has been staring at the same picture for a long period of time.

At this point, I could have come in, guns blazing, to restructure the organization as I saw fit, eliminating fat and creating a vision for the future and a painted picture in a vacuum. This is indeed what happens a lot of the time after an acquisition or when new leadership takes over. In fact, this is the very subject of my next book, the working title of which is *Surviving an Acquisition and the Assholes Involved (Hint: One of Them Might Be You)*.

As the leader, it was my job to own the vision and display the painted picture for all to see. But that didn't mean I had to create it all on my own. When I painted the picture by myself, I saw us as a $50 million business entity in four years with twice the profit margin (as a percentage of revenue) over our current rate. I saw new markets and new products and services. But I wanted the employees and the management team to feel that they had played a significant part in the development of the picture.

As a next step, I employed the services of an outside consultant, someone experienced in working with organizations to help them put together their visions and plans for achieving them. The consultant's first order of business was to interview my leadership team and me.

While she did that, I solicited suggestions from all employees. Anyone who wanted to participate by submitting thoughts and ideas for growth and improvement was welcomed and invited to do so. We provided multiple options for individuals and teams to submit their ideas, including all-employee meetings, round-table discussions, one-on-one discussions, and anonymous suggestion boxes.

The consultant gathered up all of this information, organized it, and brought it to a planning session that we had scheduled. With the consultant playing the role of facilitator, we held a weekend-long work session with all of the leaders from the company. This was not limited to managers and executives. It included anyone in any kind of a leadership position, formal or informal. We brought together all aspects of the organization, including operations, sales, human resources, finance, facilities management, and administration.

We were looking to achieve an "all-in" moment. That meant we needed everyone to be all-in, not just the executive leadership team, not just sales, and not just operations. At this meeting, everyone was equal, except for me, because I wore a cape. Just kidding.

What we walked away with that weekend was literally a painted picture. Actually, it was a series of flipcharts with pictures, words, and graphs hand-drawn with magic markers. It was crude and amateurish in places, but it painted the picture of what we envisioned the company to be a few years down the road and included in big, bold print the number "$50,000,000."

This visual aid was hung on the wall at our next all-employee meeting for everyone to see, to help us communicate the vision. This was far more effective than any document, slide presentation, or speech we could have provided them.

If I were to do it again today, I'd probably produce a cheap three- to five-minute video that did the same thing. That would be my physical representation of a painted picture, but it can take on whatever form makes the most sense for your business (and you).

■ DREAM BIG BUT HAVE SOME BASIS IN REALITY

When the inevitable questions like "That's a great vision. How are we going to get there?" came at the all-employee meeting, we would say, "I'm glad you asked."

Then we'd explain that we hadn't just created the vision and painted picture out of thin air. We had studied market opportunities, we assessed our clients' needs and wants, and, importantly, we assessed our products, services, and ability. As a result of all of this analysis, we painted a picture that had a basis in reality. After all, you wouldn't start your vacation plan by selecting Mars as your destination. Dale Hollow Lake in Tennessee may not be as exciting as a trip to Mars, but considering your budget, travel, and time constraints, it is far more realistic at this point.

It was important to show our employees that we weren't just a bunch of wild-eyed wing nuts by showing them that our vision, though aggressive, was based in reality. We had to have that for buy-in.

For this reason, before the weekend session that resulted in a painted picture, the consultant interviewed me and asked, "Why $50 million?" which is what I set as our growth target.

I still debate to this day whether my response was brilliant or idiotic, but it was, "Because I don't think I can get my people to believe we can do anything greater."

In reality, I didn't think $75 million was out of the question, but I didn't believe the organization would see that picture as anything more than make-believe. We got our employees and leaders to buy into that $50 million objective. We had successfully painted the picture, and that was absolutely critical to our path to success. But there was a period of time when I was uncertain that we would institutionalize that belief.

This was made painfully obvious when in response to the question "How do we turn this into a $50 million operation," an employee submitted the following in one of the suggestion boxes: "Why would we ever want to do that?!"

Clearly, this employee was not going to buy in to the vision or believe the picture. This, in fact, was true of a few employees, and they ultimately did not make the cut. There was no future there for them. Some left of their own accord while others were "invited to explore other opportunities." Those left standing formed a unified front, focused on making the vision a reality.

■ NOW COMES STRATEGY

When asked how we would make the painted picture a reality, the more complete answer included, "We haven't figured it all out yet. That comes next with the development and execution of a detailed plan."

Using the findings of the consultant, the input of the employees, and the honest analysis of our reality, we honed the vision and painted the picture. Next, we began to put the strategy together for achieving it. We divided up the various responsibilities and allocated them to subteams, which we intentionally populated with cross-functional knowledge in an attempt to begin to break down the barriers between different parts of the organization.

We did everything in the twelve-step method—with one major exception. We never moved off that $50 million target until we reached it. And then we did it all over again, creating a new strategy targeted at getting us to $100 million in four more years. Were I to go back in time, we would have created a three-year plan that would have been continually modified to remain a three-year plan at all times, while continuously increasing its objectives and expectations. We would have never started all over again. But otherwise we unwittingly created and followed the twelve-step process in our quest to hit $50 million.

In the end, we very nearly reached $90 million within the second four-year period, but during that time we were acquired by a much larger company. As we were assimilated into the new company, we became less and less of a cohesive organization, until eventually there was no recognizable unit remaining. Our company had been dissected and the parts moved around to other parts of the parent company (where they subsequently began to fail).

But it sure was fun while it lasted. Most of us involved had a great time and established close personal bonds that remain intact today. It is my wish that everyone have a similar experience at least once in their professional careers. What a ride!

■ A NOTE ON VISION, MISSION, AND PURPOSE

There are many books, methods, pieces of advice, rules of thumb, and processes out there dedicated to teaching you how to develop your vision and mission. This book isn't one of them. It merely emphasizes the critical importance of doing so and provides an example of how I did it on one occasion.

But worth mentioning is the difference between a mission statement and a purpose statement. The mission is what we do. The purpose is why we do it: the emotional hook. In the $50 million example, we developed what we referred to as our mission statement, as follows: "We help make the lives of those we serve just a little bit better."

Why a "little bit"? Because our services helped people who were in truly desperate situations. We couldn't possibly make a miserable situation suddenly completely hunky-dory. If a family lost their entire home and favorite pet to a flood and we provided them with a check maximizing the claim payment, we just made that family's life a little bit better...but they still have no home and their pet is gone.

The point of the statement was to inspire the employees to think beyond the fact that they were programmers, underwriters, claims examiners, and customer service representatives. They were people providing services to those who really needed them.

I have since come to appreciate that this was not our mission...it was our purpose. Our mission was to deliver P3 programs that maximized participant benefits and minimized taxpayer cost.

Graham Kenny puts it this way in his September 3, 2014, article in the *Harvard Business Review*: "If you're crafting a purpose statement, my advice is this: To inspire your staff to do good work for you, find a way to express the organization's impact on the lives of customers, clients, students, patients — whomever you're trying to serve. Make them feel it."

■ THE CHAPTER 1 WRAP

There is great power in writing things down. In this chapter, we introduced the Business Is ART framework and identified a twelve-step process for treating it as such. We then walked you through a real example and discussed the first three steps in more detail:

1. Articulate the vision.
2. Conduct a self-assessment.
3. Paint the picture.

Cameron Herold's book *Double Double* does a nice job of explaining how to paint the picture and provides the reader with a list of several questions to ask. He suggests envisioning that you have traveled three years into the future and are working around your place of business, making observations, and answering those questions to help you paint the picture.

I suggest creating a literal work of art to paint the picture, be it something that hangs on the wall, a web site, a video, a song, or anything else that tells any stakeholder exactly what you envision in a brief moment. It is important that others understand your painted picture so that they are more likely to get on board to help you realize your vision. If they don't "get it," they can't support it.

Chapter 3 will address steps four through eight of the twelve-step process, but before that, chapter 2 provides a little advice to consider before and while completing steps one through three.

Before proceeding, please take a moment to answer the following questions:

1. What is your vision?
2. What is your personal definition of success?
3. Are your business and personal visions and missions in sync?

TWO

REFUSING TO BE CONSTRAINED BY THE SHACKLES OF CHOREOGRAPHY

Following the rules of your industry
will only get you so far.
MAX MCKEOWN, *THE STRATEGY BOOK*

I hate line dancing. I hate when those two or three songs inevitably start at wedding receptions or parties, or when the karaoke DJ decides to take a break, and people get up, line up, and begin doing whatever it is they do to those songs, all in unison. I hate it.

So when people ask me why I'm not joining them, rather than be a jerk and say, "Because I think line dancing is stupid," I like to say, "Because I refuse to be constrained by the shackles of choreography." And then I chuckle and say, "That means I can't dance."

The result is that people either laugh in response or look at me as if I'm the jerk I was trying to avoid appearing to be, but inevitably they walk away and leave me alone.

The reality is I actually can dance. If I were a star, you would probably never see me on *Dancing with the Stars*, but if you did, I would likely get through a few rounds before being sent home. I would not win, but I can dance passably when I want to. I just really don't like line dancing.

It is probably more accurate to say that I don't like playing within certain boundaries. I like to be creative and play outside the boundaries. I like to play outside the box (a cliché, but it describes what I'm talking about).

When we play within the boundaries, when we only play within our defined box, if we're really playing, eventually, that box is going to get too full. When it does, we have nowhere to go. The seams stretch. It gets hard to close the top, and we just can't fit anything else in. If we try, the box breaks and everything inside comes spilling out. To keep this from happening, we need to expand our box, add a box, get a bigger box, or throw away the old content and replace it with something new. And that is exactly what some retail giants like Ikea have done.

Like most big-box retailers, Ikea uses a workforce management tool that helps the company keep track of its employees worldwide. But there's a twist: instead of looking at employees as a source of cost, which is the norm, Ikea looks at employees as a source of revenue and profit. What a concept!

The idea is to put better-paid, better-informed employees, and more of them, in the places where the customers tend to migrate. The result? Customers ask more questions that employees are better prepared to answer, leaving the customer better informed and more likely to buy. The concept pays off at both the top and bottom line (revenue and profit).

In the grand scheme of things, this isn't really thinking outside of the box. This is just going back to something that used to work. Let me explain.

Back in old Grandpappy's day, if Grandpappy wanted to build a new front porch, what did he do? He went down to the local lumber company and discussed his plans with old Clem, who owned the lumber company. Old Grandpappy could ask Clem any question about building his porch, and old Clem had the answer.

Grandpappy would leave the store with all of the materials, information, and design ideas he needed. Meanwhile, old Clem went home and had an ice-cold lemonade on the front porch, happy in knowing he'd made one more satisfied customer.

And then someone, somewhere decided this dance was getting old, threw off the shackles of choreography, and created a new dance that the kids were just crazy about: the big-box, do-it-yourself superstore. Poor old Clem couldn't keep up, so instead of handing the family business down to that spoiled, unappreciative, lazy, good-for-nothing kid of his, he sold the shop to a real estate developer, who subsequently leveled the store and lumberyard, turned the land into a residential neighborhood, and made a pile of cash. Meanwhile, old Clem took a minimum-wage job at the new big-box store stocking shelves.

Oh, every once in a while someone would ask him a question about this or that, reminding old Clem of the glory days, but not all that often. Years later, old Clem passed away. It was a beautiful ceremony. Grandpappy, of course, said a few words.

After the service and some lunch in the church basement (fried chicken and shredded beef sandwiches with a heavy side of brownies, pie, and plenty of cheap, strong coffee), you tell old Grandpappy, "Well, I have to get down to the store and pick up a few things for a new deck addition I'm building. See you later, Grandpappy. Love you."

You arrive at the store and wander up and down several aisles for a while before determining that what you need has to be in either aisle five, six, or seven. Has to be. Eventually, someone in an apron spots you and asks if you need help.

"Yes, I'm looking for those thingies you use to attach deck floor joists to the framey-like wood around the outside-ish part of the deck floor," you say.

"Um, I think you need aisle thirteen."

"Cool. Thanks!"

"No problem."

You go to aisle thirteen, can't find what you aren't sure you need, say "Screw it," which makes you think, "Hey, I have some old screws lying around; I'll just use them instead," and walk out without making a purchase.

Just to complete this story, the deck looks great, but two years later, an improperly installed floor joist gives way under old Grandpappy's chair, and he falls through, dying instantly. He is now buried in a plot next to old Clem down at Old Cedar Cemetery off old Route 62.

Personal tragedies notwithstanding, an executive at the big-box sees profits declining and wonders why. A nearby underpaid laborer says, "Hey! If I knew anything about the thingies that attach the deck floor joists to the framey-like wood thing, I could sell them for you. But I can't be everywhere at once. I got to be close to those thingies. And a little wage boost wouldn't hurt."

Old Clem's spirit whispers in the executive's ear, and the executive exclaims, "Let's do it!"

The lesson in this story is that Ikea's strategy of having better-paid, better-informed employees located where the customers migrate is not a new one. That's exactly what old Clem was to old Grandpappy back in the day. The only difference is, Ikea applied an old idea to a big-box store, proving the point that, to shed the shackles of choreography, an idea doesn't have to be new. It just has to be different than what you and everyone else have been doing.

■ DANCING ELEPHANTS

An outgrowth of having a long career is that
I have a lot of interesting things around that I get
to revisit, and, someday, get to the place where
they become something that I want to do next.
BRUCE SPRINGSTEEN

In the last chapter, I mentioned feedback from one employee who asked why we would ever want to grow the company to $50 million. Clearly, there was some line dancing going on. I took this comment as an invitation to join in, but, clearly, I was not going to. I was not going to be constrained by the shackles of choreography.

But this employee wasn't necessarily alone. Indeed, when the first big new market growth opportunity came along and we presented it to our governing board, that same question came up: "Why would we ever want to do this?"

Other questions like "What are the risks?" came up as well because what we were proposing was that we step out of the choreography that had made the company successful and learn or make up a few smooth moves of our own.

It was smart to ask the questions. It would have been foolish on our part not to have solid responses in anticipation of them. It would have been opportunity lost to let fear and conformity stop us dead in our tracks.

This is exactly what Louis Gerstner Jr. says in his book about his experience as CEO at IBM, entitled *Who Says Elephants Can't Dance?* Sometimes we have to throw off those shackles and get our groove thing on.

Gerstner's book chronicles how he, as the new CEO, championed changes at IBM, leading it from its tired old computer hardware–based business model to a service-oriented company. The service-oriented company could take advantage of the information technology world that was bursting with new software, platforms, ideas, and theories, often, if not usually, disparate from one another. IBM would become the global expert on how to make it all fit and work together. IBM would become an integrator. This was a brilliant and timely strategy.

What I liked best about the book was its chapter on culture, because it further proves the point I made about Clem and the big-box store.

For many years, the standard dress code for corporate America was the dark suit, white shirt, and tie. There was once a time when my closet was full of them. But one day, the media announced rather loudly that IBM, under Gerstner's leadership, was changing its dress code. They were abandoning the suit and tie and going to business casual. It seemed as if it only took a few days from that announcement until nearly all big companies in the United States were following suit (pun intended). Everyone was going to business casual, and Gerstner was seen as a trailblazer (more puns).

But what most of us didn't know until reading his book was that Gerstner wasn't really coming up with a trailblazing idea, he was simply removing the shackles of choreography and revisiting an old idea.

Legendary IBM leader Thomas J. Watson established the dark suit and tie dress code for IBM—the dress code that really defined the dress code for corporate America for decades—simply because he noticed that was how the buyers dressed. His code wasn't so much, "You must wear a dark suit, white shirt, and tie," as, according to Gerstner, "Respect your customer and dress accordingly."

Gerstner simply noticed that his buyers were dressing more casually and reemployed Watson's notion: respect your customer and dress accordingly. The dress code itself had become the shackles. Gerstner merely removed them, thereby sending khaki stock through the roof. Now we all look like shoe salesmen (thanks, Louis), and, in fact, what started as IBM's refusal to continue to be constrained by the shackles of choreography has now become a new set of shackles: business casual. But in this case, there are just so many ways we can dress ourselves for work, so a little bit of shackling isn't always a bad thing.

■ RADICAL CHANGE

Sometimes throwing off the shackles takes more than merely rehashing something old. Sometimes it means coming up with something entirely new, representing radical change. My youngest daughter, Abigail, helped with some of the research for this book. On the topic of "Refusing to Be Constrained by the Shackles of Choreography," she said this:

> In my music education class, my professor started talking about time periods and how, for a very long time, music was a sure pattern. It was structured and, though always a different tune, a different formation of notes and rhythms, the pattern was always palpable. But as time went on and impressionism emerged in the art world, artists like Monet and Renoir started painting pictures that, to quote Dr. Tipps directly, "looked as if you were looking at the picture through a sort of fog," and that carried itself into music. The tunes became opaque and sort of just ended on an unresolved chord or abruptly. It stuck out to me simply because of the

dramatic switch between absolute clarity to "fog" and, well, sort of obscurity and fuzziness, if you will.

Why did Monet, his colleague Renoir, and a few other notable artists create impressionism? Simply put, in Monet's case, he became disillusioned with what was taught in traditional art schools, so he threw off the shackles and created something radically different.

It's fascinating how one form of art, impressionist painting, inspired a movement in another form of art: musical impressionism. In music, the impressionist movement is largely viewed as a rejection of the romantic music of the time, which in turn was related to romanticism in painting and literature. The shackles of romanticism were thrown off in order to create radical change. The same is often true in business and makes a great, albeit unintended, point that's relevant to Business Is ART: when you create one work of art, you never know what other art it will inspire, and if you keep creating, the possibilities become endless.

Henry Ford created his automobile, which led to automobile assembly lines. Competitors saw his "black cars only" option and created a new work of art, recognizing a market opportunity in offering colors other than black. Ned Compton invented the "Comp"-uter, which inspired former United States Vice President Al Gore to invent the Internet: neither of which is true, but you get the point. If art imitates life, then art inspires art and, in turn, inspires how we live, which inspires art to imitate life: a complete circle that when spun wildly enough, produces radical change.

■ NO SHACKLES WITH NO PLAN
  IS A WASTE OF TIME

So how does one remove the shackles? Unless you are just naturally prone to going against the grain, throwing off the shackles begins with the honest assessment of yourself discussed in chapter 1 and the honest assessment of your organization, which will be discussed in chapter 3. When you can honestly look at things and yourself, it should become readily clear what is working and what is not. You begin to imagine what is holding you back and what life would be like without those constraints.

And then you do something bold. You decide to no longer let those shackles constrain you. But you still have to have a plan!

Let's look at things literally for a moment. Imagine a prison inmate, in shackles, working on a road crew alongside a busy highway. Somehow, some way, this prisoner has devised a key to unlock the shackles. He waits for the right moment, when the guards are otherwise occupied, and unlocks and removes the shackles. And then he just stands there. He's got no plan. He's got nowhere to run. He's got no one driving by to pick him up.

Soon, a guard notices, points his rifle at the unshackled prisoner, and says, "Put those back on, you big dummy."

Socially disturbing example? OK, I will grant you that. But you get the picture, right? Once you have determined to throw off the shackles of choreography, devise a plan for what you will do when the shackles are removed...*before* removing them except in the case of emergency. You have to have a plan and be thoroughly committed to change, or you aren't going anywhere.

"But this stuff doesn't just come to me. My brain doesn't work that way," you might say.

Just remember, any plan is ART and anyone can be an ARTist. We just all have different methods. So find or create one that works for you. Here are some suggestions to help you along:

1. **Take time out.** Set aside time to remove yourself from the shackled environment to just kind of free your mind. That could be literally or figuratively. Maybe an afternoon on the water. Maybe a walk on the bike path. Maybe yoga. Maybe a treadmill. Maybe lying down on your couch with no TV or distractions. Whatever works for you. I personally have to work at finding ways to make my mind just shut down for a while. Not thinking is one of the hardest things to do because there is always something going on up there. But I find some of my best ideas come to me in the shower, riding in silence in the car, floating on a boat, or at that point between being asleep and waking up in the morning: those times when my mind is not racing on any number of subjects.

2. **Brainstorm.** Now, some people think the term "brainstorming" is old, tired, irrelevant, and even politically incorrect. The cool kids are trying out all kinds of alternative words for it, like "mind showers." But it's a fruitless religious argument. Call it whatever you want; it's how you do it that matters. The one thing you want to avoid is "groupthink." This is when the most vocal or senior people in the room dominate the idea-generation session and, due to either their volume

or their title, everyone else becomes robotic and automatically says, "That's a great idea." Find a way that works for you and your group in which all voices are heard and all ideas at least get on the table for consideration. For me, that method is the trusty old yellow sticky pad, for two reasons. One, it gives everyone a voice, and two, as previously stated, there is tremendous power in writing something down. A method you might try is to hand out yellow sticky pads to everyone and ask them to write single ideas on single pieces of paper for whatever the topic or question is. Set a time limit. I like one to three minutes, depending on what I have asked them to respond to. Then tell them "pens down" and collect it all. Now you can stick all the ideas up on the wall and even begin to categorize them before moving on to the next topic. This works for me, but you have to find whatever works best for you. Maybe it's this. Maybe not.

3. **Reverse engineer.** In *Double Double*, Herold suggests starting with the end state in mind, then working your way backward to determine the path forward. Instead of saying, "First, I need this," think, "Last, I need this. Right before it, I need that." Go from point Z to point A rather than points A to Z in your planning process to avoid the trap of doing the same old things the same old ways, hoping you will get different results. J.D. Salinger said, "I am a kind of paranoid in reverse. I suspect people of plotting to make me happy." While there is humor in this statement, it is also very profound and perfectly parallels what Herold is saying. Salinger's destination in

this case is people making him happy. Narcissistic? Maybe. Selfish? Perhaps. Clever statement? Definitely. He starts with the destination. So what is he likely to do? He is likely to start from that destination and consciously or unconsciously work his way backward, ultimately engaging and surrounding himself only with those people who make him happy.

4. **Don't "exception handle."** It drives me crazy when we're trying to figure something out and there is that one person in the room who constantly says, "Well, that only works if this is true." Pretty soon, we are so deep down a rabbit hole that even the rabbit has to carry an oxygen tank. So if you can't go from Z to A and just have to go from A to Z, then stay focused on getting to Z by assuming everything will work just fine. You can exception handle on the next few passes, but on the first go, just go.

■ THE SHACKLES ARE DEVELOPING FASTER AND FASTER

In April 2011, Evan Spiegel presented the idea of Snapchat to his collegiate product design class. The other students did not think it was such a great idea. This was a generation already constrained by the shackles of a relatively new choreography: Facebook.

The idea for Snapchat was to provide a vehicle to post photos and messages momentarily versus "permanently." Instead of building photo albums and posts on your account that last until you delete them and may still be "out there" if someone downloads or saves them, Snapchat would offer something more like a real, in-person conversation. Show it or say it, and a few seconds later, it's gone. If you were there and heard it or saw it, you heard or saw it. But if you weren't, it's just hearsay, rumor, and scuttlebutt. Like the spoken word, it fades into the ether. The memory of those words may last and reverberate, but they are never to be heard in that moment ever again.

Once again, this isn't a particularly new idea. All of us have conversations that are meant to be private. Most or all of us have conversations that are meaningless chitchat that we don't particularly want to document in historical records. It's just talking. And that's really what Snapchat is. But for it to be invented, the founders had to remove the shackles of other social media sites like Facebook in order to create the Snapchat picture.

What's remarkable about the IBM dress code story and the Snapchat story is the speed with which the shackles develop. It took decades for one, and a few short years for the other. This trend will likely continue as technology advances. My prediction is that there will be very few truly new ideas, merely new methods for reinventing stuff we have always done. Nonetheless, we have to continually remove the shackles of choreography and invent or reinvent new moves.

■ STAYING RELEVANT

*The thing is with hip-hop, it has its waves and the
waves crash against the beach and the new waves come in.
So to stay relevant you have to roll with that.*
ICE CUBE, ENTERTAINER

Refusing to be constrained by the shackles of choreography means staying relevant. It means rolling with the new waves that crash onto the beach. But how does one do that? Again, some people seem to be born with a predisposition to it. For others, it's a discipline, but it's something most of us can do. Here are some suggestions for remaining relevant:

1. Don't get comfortable. Jon Bon Jovi said, "Don't get too comfortable with who you are at any given time—you may miss the opportunity to become who you want to be." There's nothing like a nice bed or a comfortable couch to stretch out on and snuggle on for a while to watch a movie or your favorite team. But don't let life be that couch. If you do, you'll fall asleep while everyone and everything changes around you. When you wake up, you may even find that someone took the remote.

2. Pay attention! Things are constantly changing. Particularly in business, if you aren't paying attention, you will become irrelevant in relatively short order. Going back to the $50 million business example, when I took it over, one of the people responsible for one of the pieces of the business told me that for that particular market, the Internet was irrelevant. Clients were asking for web-based software, but it provided them with no real benefit, so they didn't need it, so we weren't going to give it to them. The client–server solution provided all they'd ever realistically need. Hence, there were no plans to develop a

web-based solution. This notion sort of horrified me. Was it true that a web-based solution offered no real benefit to the customer? Possibly. Did that matter? Not at all.

If you find yourself saying, "The customers aren't asking for it and don't need it," you probably need to rethink your strategy, and more likely, you don't have one.

Andy Warhol said, "An artist is somebody who produces things that you don't need to have."

Truly great innovators create things consumers didn't even know they needed but now can't live without. Not shockingly, we don't really need them in the greatest sense of the word, but the innovator convinces us that we do. Before long, we prove their point for them.

Steve Jobs was a master and an exceptional artist in this regard. Among his many accomplishments, he turned the computer into a work of art. Sleek, attractive, colorful designs are now the norm, but they weren't until Jobs, the artist, inspired their creation. Today, a computer might be the fastest, most powerful and useful one on the market. But if it comes in a gray metal box with sharp corners, you will immediately think to yourself that it is an old, obsolete system. You don't need sleekness and prettiness, but you think you do.

And can you imagine your life without a mobile device? You feel naked without it. Incomplete. Out of touch and isolated. Yet not so long ago in the history of the human, only a privileged few had them. Just a few years before that, no one did.

But unless you are in it for that one-time big-bang payback, innovation has to continue to occur, ever more rapidly, in order to stay relevant. Look at the BlackBerry. The what? Exactly. It came on hot in the market as the go-to business mobile phone and email device, but it failed to reinvent itself in the time frame that others like Apple and Android did. The BlackBerry rotted in the bowl. No one likes a bowl full of rotten blackberries. You can quote me on that.

■ IMPLORE TO EXPLORE

> *Exploration is the engine that drives*
> *innovation. Innovation drives economic growth.*
> *So let's all go exploring.*
> EDITH "EDIE" WIDDER, AMERICAN OCEANOGRAPHER

Exploration is vital to innovation, and it starts with asking a simple question: What if? When we created our $50 million picture, we asked several "what if" questions.

· What if we focus on services?
· What if we do this by playing to our technological strength?
· What if we create things the customers don't know they need?
· What if we don't get into price wars with our closest competitors?
· What if we take this solution and service from that market and apply them to another?

Exploration doesn't start with knowing where the bodies are buried or where the ship sank. It starts with the notion that the bodies and the ship are out there, and I'm going to find them!

ROBERT BALLARD, EXPLORER

Robert Ballard is credited with leading the team that eventually found the *Titanic*. Finding the wreckage was far from an overnight success: it was a continual story of creating innovative solutions, using previous ideas in new, innovative ways, and using the inventions of others. Sometimes success is defined by determining that what you thought might work has proven to not work at all. By process of elimination, you find what does work.

When we explore, we say to the world, "I don't care what you think you know." People thought the *Titanic* would never be found. But with a will and a willingness to innovate, Ballard found it.

Ballard has said, "I'm a geophysicist, and [in] all my earth science books when I was a student, I had to give the wrong answer to get an A. We used to ridicule continental drift. It was something we laughed at. We learned of Marshall Kay's geosynclinal cycle, which is a bunch of crap."

This quote is so far over my head that even Microsoft Word doesn't recognize the term "geosynclinal." But his message is plain and simple. Don't accept it just because it is the norm. Don't be constrained by the shackles of choreography. Explore!

If I had listened to the former executive who said that the customer didn't need a web-based solution, we would have missed opportunities that amounted to approximately $20 million per year in annual revenue by the time I left the company. Instead, we chose to explore: we asked, "What if the customer feels the need for it? What if we provide it?"

■ THE CHAPTER 2 WRAP

In this chapter, we stepped away from process (science) for a bit and focused on the art of freestyle dancing. We discussed how some people have thrown off the shackles of choreography and in so doing have sometimes created a brand new dance step. But often we are reapplying or reinventing a move created long, long ago. Throwing off the shackles of choreography is necessary to stay relevant, but a willingness and desire to do so are not enough. You also have to have a plan for how to proceed once the shackles have been removed. It does no good to throw off the shackles only to stand there and wait for someone to slap them back on.

Sometimes it takes a willingness to explore in order to figure out how to throw off the shackles of choreography. You have to try applying old solutions to new problems. You have to try applying new solutions to new problems. And you have to try applying new solutions to old problems. But the important thing is to try and to take calculated risks.

In chapter 3, we return to the twelve-step approach, addressing steps four through eight.

Before proceeding, please answer the following questions:

1. What shackles do you wear (what is holding you back)?
2. Can you think of a time when you threw off the shackles?
3. If so, what motivated you to do so, and did you have a plan when you did it?

THREE

STRATEGIC PLANNING

Strategy 101 is about choices:
You can't be all things to all people.
MICHAEL PORTER

Let's talk about strategic planning: what it is and what it's not. This chapter covers three aspects of the topic: some general thoughts on planning, the definition of strategic planning, and some characteristics of a strategic plan.

First, some general thoughts, and speaking of generals, Dwight D. Eisenhower said, "Plans are nothing; planning is everything."

To achieve the mission, we must plan. We often don't like it. We'd rather not do it. It sometimes seems like a waste of time. But if we jump right into things without a plan, the mission will fail or not be as successful as it could have been.

Another saying that I like is that we plan to manage, but we manage the plan. This is another way of saying the same thing that General Eisenhower said. It means that we establish a plan in order to manage objectives, but we have to be smart enough and flexible enough to expect and anticipate changes.

So what is strategic planning? When I looked around online for definitions of strategic planning, I kept finding references to things like "focusing resources," "establishing agreement," and "assessing and adjusting the organization's response." I found arguments for and against using the phrase "execute the strategy." I found blog posts too long to even skim through written by people who referred to themselves as "strategy wonks." There is not enough coffee in Colombia to keep anyone awake long enough to muddle through the volumes of definition and opinions.

I like to think of strategic planning simply as identifying and then acting on the things you need to do to reach your vision. One sip of coffee is all you need to let that definition sink in.

Strategic planning is a disciplined effort that produces fundamental decisions and actions that shape and guide what an organization is, who it serves, what it does, and why it does it—all with a focus on the future.

Simply put, it is the discipline to look before we leap. And it really is a discipline.

When my son was in day care, his teacher conducted the Stanford marshmallow experiment, which involves marshmallows and the promise of more marshmallows to come. Each child is given a choice: eat one marshmallow now and get none later or wait fifteen minutes and get two marshmallows.

A small minority waited for two, but most of the children aged five and under ate the one marshmallow now because they couldn't conceptualize the meaning of "fifteen minutes from now."

Unfortunately, that is how many managers, executives, and business organizations think and behave as well (way past the age of five). Too often we want one marshmallow now, even knowing that if we just wait a little bit we will get two marshmallows. This can be especially true in publicly traded companies where the emphasis is on returns now versus a year from now. Too often this rewards short-term behaviors for short-term gains at the cost of long-term success.

In this kind of environment, it's very difficult not just to have a strategic plan, but to think and behave strategically. (In fairness to my son, I honestly think he understood the concept of "one now, none later" versus "none now, two later"; I believe he was just so sure of himself that he thought he'd have one now and figure out a way to get another one later.)

So what is a strategic plan? The strategic plan is a document to communicate with the organization: it describes the organization's goals, the actions needed to achieve those goals, and all the other critical elements developed during the planning exercise.

Note that having a strategic plan and doing strategic planning is not the same as strategic management. We will discuss strategic management in more detail in the next chapter. However, in the meantime you can think of strategic management as those things we do to execute the plan.

There are many different frameworks and methodologies for strategic planning and management. Most of these methodologies follow a similar pattern and have common attributes. Many frameworks cycle through some variation on the following basic phases:

1. The analysis or assessment phase: developing an understanding of the current internal and external environment.
2. The strategy formulation phase: developing high-level strategy and documenting a basic organization-level strategic plan.
3. The strategic execution phase: translating the high-level plan into more operational planning and action items.
4. The evaluation or sustainment/management phase: ongoing evaluation and refinement.

Most organizations never get to phases three and four. In my own experience, most organizations never get to phase two, leaving them in a constant phase one discussion that never ends and never achieves any results, other than the consumption of a lot of pizza and boxed lunches: tasty, but not what you needed.

I once worked for a company that insisted that every division have a strategic plan, which would roll up to the corporate-level plan. Great idea, but thick with problems, the first one being that no one had any idea what the corporate strategy was or whether their divisional strategy fit in with it. The second problem was that the strategic plan smelled a lot more like a one-year business plan than a multiyear strategy. A third problem was that the "strategy" template we had to use focused on big, lofty goals but included no place to identify measurable objectives.

Finally, the process for reviewing the strategies after the initial submissions did not exist. It was up to each division to carry through. How successful do you think those strategies were? If you guessed "not at all," you guessed right. The "strategic plans" were nothing more than an exercise to satisfy someone somewhere that everyone had a strategy. Once delivered, those documents were forgotten, and it was right back to business as usual, which, in this case, meant focusing on today's delivery and revenue recognition while ignoring tomorrow.

Not only was there no plan execution or follow-up, I'd argue that effectively, there was no plan to begin with.

As an executive and a consultant, I've run across numerous business owners and leaders who bristle when I make comments like "The vast majority of businesses operate without a plan."

A common response is, "Well, I have a plan. It's not a formal plan, and most of it's in my head, but I have a plan."

They don't have a plan. They have a thought. Until it moves from your mind to the canvas, you don't have art. Until you move to the canvas, you can't follow ART. Andy Warhol never had an exhibit consisting of all empty walls and entitled "Stuff I'm Thinking about Painting." Unless you've committed your plans to some physical medium, you don't have a plan.

When "plans" remain encapsulated in the mind, and nowhere else, here are some of the likely outcomes:

- You might get lucky and do just fine. But are your business, your livelihood, the livelihoods of your employees, and your vision worth leaving to chance? If so, then by all means, knock yourself out. After all, the best strategy in the history of mankind cannot guarantee success. But there is a pretty good chance that without it, failure or less than the full realization of success will occur. It's just a matter of when and how bad it will be.

- You will have several "flathead" moments. That's when you slap your forehead with the palm of your hand and say, "I should have seen that coming," possibly using some naughty words as substitutes for full sentences.

- You are the only one who knows your vision. If no one else knows it, you're on your own. No one can help you achieve it if they don't know or understand it. Commit the plan to some form of media so that others can see exactly where you are headed and can help you get there. You don't have to go it alone.

There is tremendous power in writing things down. It almost feels like magic. Maybe it is magic. Maybe when you write things down you are saying to the universe, "This is what I want. Won't you help me get there?" And the universe responds in kind. Maybe in writing it down, it becomes more real to you (and others). "OK, this isn't just an idea anymore. I've written it down, so now I *have* to do it." Maybe it's no more complicated than this: if you don't write it down, you'll forget it. Just don't forget to write it down.

Let's define the major components of a strategic plan first by dispelling some myths.

■ COMMON MYTHS ABOUT STRATEGIC PLANNING

1. A strategic plan can only exist at the organization or company level.
2. A strategic plan must look out more than five years.
3. A strategic plan is only good if it is several pages long.
4. A strategic plan has a defined completion date.
5. A strategic initiative is the same thing as a strategy.

Myth 1: A Strategic Plan Can Only Exist at the Organization or Company Level
Not only is this wrong, it is also foolhardy. Strategies and strategic plans can exist at any level, including the team and individual contributor levels. The key is to ensure that each lower-level strategy or strategic plan ties directly to the strategy at the next higher level.

Myth 2: A Strategic Plan Must Look Out More than Five Years
No one has invented an accurate and reliable crystal ball to date as far as I know. As rapidly as culture, business environment, technology, and other factors change, it is impossible for anyone to look accurately far into the future even when historical models might suggest

otherwise. My recommendation is that your strategic plan looks out no further than you can reasonably envision the future (i.e., paint the picture) and that it covers a maximum of three years.

Myth 3: A Strategic Plan Is Only Good
If It Is Several Pages Long
Through the years, my thoughts on strategic plans have been refined. I once was responsible for putting together a strategic plan for the CIO (chief information officer) of a major insurance company. This CIO was a grand thinker and truly visionary. He did everything big. So it would stand to reason that any strategy he had in mind for his $150 million information technology department would also be big.

And so to make a long story short, when my efforts to put together his strategy were complete, we were left with several three-inch binders plus a video that cost tens of thousands of dollars and starred the CIO, sometimes in a suit and sometimes in his bike team uniform. Sweet!

This strategy thought of everything. And it was exceptionally effective. It was exceptionally effective at making this CIO feel good about himself. It was exceptionally effective at gathering dust. It was completely ineffective at actually helping the organization to get anything done.

But I learned my lesson. Going back to the $50 million example, when we put the strategy together, I applied what I had learned from the experience of developing a monolithic, useless strategic plan and scaled things back.

Instead of multiple three-inch binders, we developed multiple half-inch binders. That saves 2.5 inches for every binder. Even so, they contained too much "junk." The "junk" was pages and pages of detailed descriptions of the market or of a service. No one was going to read that.

Anybody who had opened up a binder and looked at all of that script would immediately have said, "Hey, who wants to go have a cheeseburger?" As soon as someone said, "Me," they would have put down the binder and never returned, which would have been sad, because in addition to the junk, there was some really good stuff in there. It just was hard to find.

The acronym KISS, or "keep it simple, stupid," is way overplayed, and I cringe whenever I hear people say that they subscribe to the KISS theory (unless they are talking about the band, in which case, I too wanna rock 'n' roll all night and party every day). But I do appreciate the sentiment and agree with it. So much so that I have become a big fan of brief strategies. For this reason, I've developed a one-page strategic plan template that is available to you just for buying this book. There is nothing earth-shattering or new about this template. There are many one- and two-page templates available. It really wouldn't be very difficult for you to develop one of your own. But I am also a big fan of not reinventing the wheel, so my template is available for you.

Myth 4: A Strategic Plan Has a Defined Completion Date
This is kind of an old-school way of thinking. The grandiose strategic plans we used to put together also included very specific start and end dates. At the plan's

end date we would declare victory or defeat, start all over again, or decide we were too exhausted and not prepared to take on another strategic plan.

The aforementioned CIO's predecessor had a grandiose strategy, and we will use the term "strategy" loosely here. The strategy was to replace the old systems with a new, enterprise-wide system. But when the defined end date of the strategic plan was reached and the enterprise-wide system was nowhere near complete, both he and the strategy were declared failures. Subsequently he was replaced with his successor who developed a grandiose strategy of his own, throwing away more than $50 million from the previous software implementation effort.

But what everyone failed to understand was that the strategy was not a strategy at all. A strategy looks out over a prescribed period of time. As mentioned, I like three years as a window because it is too hard to look further than that into the future. But a strategy is ongoing and constantly evolving. Unless you are planning an exit strategy, your business doesn't end in three years, so why would your strategic plan?

Again, a strategy communicates the vision, goals, and objectives. It also includes initiatives you will undertake to make that vision a reality. Not all projects are strategic initiatives, but all strategic initiatives are projects.

In the case of replacing the old systems, the vision was really for a technological platform that provided the business with a competitive advantage. Part of the strategy was to establish a technological platform that could easily adapt to change (i.e., stay relevant). Replacing the legacy systems with a big, shiny, new enterprise-wide system was not a strategy. It was really an initiative, and not a very good one at that.

If this "big bang" replacement had been assessed against what should have been the strategy as defined in the previous paragraph, it might have been evident that the initiative did not meet the goals of the strategy because the plan was to replace the legacy systems with another system that could not keep up with and adapt to further technological advances. In other words, the plan was to replace several obsolete systems with one big, soon-to-be obsolete system. Does that sound like a good plan to you?

But even if it had been a good, solid initiative, that's all it was. It was an exceptionally large and risky initiative, but it was an initiative nonetheless, which leads us to the next myth.

Myth 5: A Strategic Initiative Is the Same Thing as a Strategy

In my experience, most leaders confuse strategic initiatives with strategy. But there is a clear difference: a strategy includes one to many strategic initiatives. A strategic initiative is basically a project with defined start and end dates as well as defined objectives.

I am in a networking group with a man who owns several fried chicken franchises. Let's call him "Joe." If Joe discovers a deep fryer that can fry the chicken in half the time, producing a more flavorful and juicy piece of chicken, then he will probably want to install that fryer in each of his franchise locations as quickly as he can.

In this example, Joe might be tempted to say, "My strategy is to install this super new fryer in all of my locations this year."

But is that really his strategy? I would contend that it is not a strategy. His vision may be to become the number-one fried chicken franchise in the region. His strategy for achieving this may be for his brand to become synonymous with fried chicken. One of his objectives supporting this strategy may be to improve customer satisfaction by 25 percent.

One of the strategic initiatives supporting this strategic objective may be to install new fryers. Objectives of this initiative may include: 1) complete the installation in all locations by the end of the calendar year, 2) reduce fry time by 50 percent, and 3) improve flavor by 15 percent (as measured by customer survey response).

Strategic plan and strategic initiative: not the same, and now that you know the difference, let's go back to the Business Is ART process and look more closely at steps four through eight, which again are:

4. Revise or refine the vision if necessary.
5. Honestly assess today's reality versus tomorrow's vision.
6. Recognize the gaps between the vision and today's reality.
7. Identify goals that you will have to meet in order to close the gap, and define objectives that will measure the rate of success in achieving those goals.

8. Identify specific initiatives, projects, or actions that have to be taken to realize those objectives.

■ REVISE OR REFINE THE VISION AS NECESSARY

Once we completed the planning session and painted the picture for our $50 million organization, it was time to take a step back, make sure we had a believable picture, and make any adjustments necessary.

In our exercise, we had unique, cross-functional teams that focused on detailed planning for each of the markets we were targeting, as well as teams focused on the company itself. When we brought all of these detailed plans together and tallied up individual market estimates, it actually came to about $53 million in potential annual revenue, so our vision didn't need a lot of revision. But this won't always be the case. We, by happenstance, landed on financial projections that really fit our initial vision. Be prepared for that to *not* be the case.

For example, the next time we put a lot of focus into a new, multiyear strategy, we targeted $100 million in revenue, but that number was derived largely out of pressure and cockiness. When we honestly assessed things, it did not appear that $100 million would be possible because there were too many constraints outside of our control. But we didn't go back and revise the new strategic plan, and I think one of the results was that we didn't feel as successful that time around, even though we got very close to $90 million.

In the $50 million example, even though our vision didn't change much, we did continue to refine the painted picture because we had other things to consider, like "Where will we put all of the additional employees we need?" and "What do we want the industry and our competitors to say about us?" You know, small details like that.

Some additional food for thought: when projecting future finances, don't assume that 100 percent of the identified targets will result in a 100 percent close rate 100 percent of the time at 100 percent of the projected revenue. As I mentioned, some time after we went through our initial growth strategy, the company was acquired by a multibillion dollar, global company, and it drove me absolutely bonkers that this was the expectation.

It subsequently drove my team to stop fully and honestly identifying pipeline opportunities, which led to the new company thinking our pipeline was weak. This in turn led to bad decisions about the sales team and delivery resources we needed to continue to be successful, which led to an inevitable decline in sales, growth, and customer satisfaction. We actually went backward from that point forward. It was a horrible, horrible situation.

A better approach is simply this:

1. Identify true pipeline opportunities.
2. Estimate the total contract value and annual revenue that would be associated with winning the account.
3. Assign a probability factor to winning the account (don't go crazy: it can be as simple as 25 percent,

50 percent, and 75 percent…never, ever assign a 100 percent probability to an opportunity; use 90 percent maximum).

4. Apply the probability factor to the total contract value and annual revenue estimates associated with the account.

5. Make that your finance projection for the account.

For example, if xyz account is worth $1 million per year, and you think you have a 25 percent chance of winning it, your financial projection should be $250,000 per year, not $1 million.

Now let's say you have four of these opportunities. Odds are if you have four opportunities with a 25 percent chance of winning, you're going to nail at least one of them but not all. So in this simple scenario, your total annual revenue projection is $1 million ($250,000 × 4 opportunities, each worth $1 million but with only a 25 percent chance of winning). Just because your pipeline says you are chasing $4 million in revenue, don't fall into the trap of equating that to a revenue projection of $4 million, unless you are running a monopoly on a product or service that everyone simply must have. Like peanut M&Ms. And beer.

Revise your financial projections accordingly as you get closer to winning and closing the deal (or losing it). In the end, if you are being honest about opportunities and your chances of winning them, the law of averages will play out and your projections will more closely mirror reality.

▣ HONESTLY ASSESS TODAY'S SITUATION

> *Integrity is telling myself the truth.*
> *And honesty is telling the truth to other people.*
> SPENCER JOHNSON, AUTHOR OF *WHO MOVED MY CHEESE?*

I once worked for a CEO who liked to say, "No one wants to admit that their baby is ugly."

That can be very true in business. We are all very skilled and experienced at putting the following types of things in our proposals and advertisements:

- We are simply the best.
- There can be no doubt that we are the best choice.
- Our service is far superior.

No one ever says, "Well, look, we ain't bad—sure, we've got a few flaws here and there, and yes, we could stand to invest in some redesign, but, hey, if it ain't broke, don't fix it, know what I mean?" in their ads and proposals.

And no one expects us to. Frankly, aside from being a wordy, run-on sentence demonstrating poor command of the English language, it is not exactly a winning message.

But when we don't admit to ourselves internally that perhaps our baby is not the pretty, pretty princess we'd like her to be, we get into trouble. We have to critically and honestly look at how ugly our baby is because we have the ability to pretty that little monster up a bit.

When we painted the $50 million picture, we did so at first without regard for exactly how we would get there.

But in the detailed planning that followed, we laid out several road maps. In some cases, we needed a complete overhaul of a system. In other cases, we needed to first admit we needed fresh, new talent.

In no case did we rest on our laurels and say, "Well, this has always worked in the past, so let's keep doing it."

But it wasn't all bad either. We had some pretty solid foundations. After all, this had been a successful company for twenty-five years. So we looked with integrity and honesty at the good as well, and then looked at how to make the good even better.

■ RECOGNIZE THE GAPS AND IDENTIFY THE GOALS AND OBJECTIVES

Steps six through eight of the twelve-step process go hand-in-hand. Once we honestly assessed the situation, we could intelligently analyze the gaps between today's situation and tomorrow's painted picture. In the analysis, we had to determine the goals that would have to be met in order to close the gap and the objectives associated with each goal.

We won't get into any big, hairy discussions about big, hairy, audacious goals (BHAG) or simple, measurable, achievable, realistic, and time-based (SMART) objectives in this book. No, no. We are going to BHAG being SMART here. Instead we will be DUMB. Don't use my book (DUMB) for that stuff because volumes of material about it exist elsewhere.

But it is vital that you identify your gaps, goals, and the objectives. In our $50 million example, one of the gaps was that in a particular industry we had a great software solution but no associated business services, even though we saw huge growth potential.

The lack of business services was the gap. One of the goals for closing the gap was to take advantage of the chaos that existed at that time in the industry and use the strength of the software to make a foray into business services. One of the objectives was to attract at least three industry subject-matter experts with strong reputations in that particular market. These people would be pegged as primary leaders in our business service offering.

Without investing any money on the business service side just yet, we then had a go-to-market strategy that used the strength of the software, the reputable strength of a leadership team that would be involved in the business services operation, and messaging that exploited the chaotic state of the industry.

In essence, we were saying, "Things are a mess. We have the technology and we have the people to bring structure and clarity to the chaos." It worked.

■ IDENTIFY STRATEGIC INITIATIVES

There have been several points made leading to a discussion on strategic initiatives, but the most important are these:

1. Strategic initiatives are not strategic plans (know the difference).
2. Many leaders do not know the difference.

Additional important points are these:

1. Don't have more than three strategic initiatives going on at any particular point in time. It is difficult to focus on more than that at once, and often impossible to fund them all. Just because something is a smart thing to do overall, doesn't mean that it is the best thing to do right now.

2. Don't limit yourself to identifying only three strategic initiatives. **Identify all that you can think of**, but before proceeding to the execution phase, see the previous point. **Prioritize and focus.**

3. **Just because it's a smart thing to do doesn't make it a strategic initiative.** For example, maybe your software release process is not working well and you are in the software business. Fix it! That's not a strategic initiative, that's just not running your business like a ninny.

4. Strategic initiatives have **defined start and end dates**.

5. Strategic initiatives **are assigned to and "owned by" someone**, emphasis on "one." Someone has to be accountable for it.

6. All strategic initiatives must connect with at least one strategic objective (and goal).

7. A strategic initiative can support multiple strategic goals and objectives.

8. A strategic initiative must have at least one SMART objective itself.

9. It is at the strategic initiative level that detailed project planning occurs, for **strategic initiatives are, indeed, projects**. The strategy is not a project. A strategic initiative is.

▪ COMMON ELEMENTS OF A STRATEGIC PLAN

Now let's look at some of the most common elements of a strategic plan. Not by coincidence, these are the same elements you will find on the one-page strategic plan template. They are as follows:

- Organization
- Date
- Version
- Vision
- Today's situation
- Strategic goals
- Strategic objectives
- Today's reality (corresponding indicators)
- Strategic initiative
- Supports strategic objective number
- Strategic initiative owner
- Strategic initiative due by
- Strategic initiative objectives

Each element will be discussed individually. The first three fields are for information purposes. They really comprise the header section of the strategic plan. In the "Organization" field, identify the company, organization within the company, product, service, project, team, or person that the strategy applies to. The "Date" field is the date the strategy was created or last modified. The "Version" field is used for version control. Remember, the strategic plan is ever-changing, so if your plan continuously says "Version 1.0," then you are doing something wrong.

The next two fields are critically important to developing your strategic plan and to managing strategically. In the "Vision" field, use as much space as you need to, but try to be brief. The idea is to make a statement that is instantly clear to the reader.

In the "Today's situation" field, provide an honest assessment of today's situation as opposed to the vision. Be brief. Remember, we are not looking for a novel here. But it is vitally important that you be honest with yourself and with the reader.

The gap between your vision and today's situation is where you want to focus your attention. Do this by identifying strategic goals that when achieved will close the gap. You may identify as many goals as you like, but I recommend no more than three to four strategic goals at a time.

Think about this in terms of your own ability to focus. Studies have shown that most human beings can only effectively focus on two to not more than five things at a time. Apply this same logic to business. When a business or organization attempts to focus on too many things, all of those things suffer.

The temptation to do more is great because in our "instant" society, we want things done and we want them done now. But some things still take time.

For example, until someone develops a way to bake delicious, moist, chewy brownies in one minute instead of 28 to 30, it's best to let them bake as usual. Have you ever had a microwaved brownie-in-a-mug? If so, I rest my case.

■ THE ProCESS STRATEGY

To develop a strategy, you have to be an artist. It requires imagination, creativity, and intuition. But even the true artist follows a process, formally or informally. For example, a painter might follow a process like this:

· Determine the subject and setting
· Study the subject and setting
· Determine the medium to use
· Study the subject and setting some more, taking the medium into consideration
· Draft a sketch
· Begin painting

I say this acknowledging that Farrah Fawcett took off her clothes, threw paint all over her naked body, rolled and scooted around on a blank canvas, took a shower, and called it art. Fine. But she still had a process.

Developing a strategy is a process and that said, I am suggesting you create a ProCESS Strategy. A ProCESS Strategy includes four major areas of focus (goals), as follows:

· **Pro**fitability
· **C**ustomer satisfaction
· **E**mployee **s**atisfaction
· **S**ocial responsibility

I would argue that pretty much any business strategic goal will fit neatly into one or more of these categories.

Social responsibility is optional, but studies are showing that it is not just a cost or a "feel good" thing to do. Companies are beginning to prove that the right corporate social responsibility programs increase profitability, so I strongly suggest it.

■ THE ONE-PAGE STRATEGIC PLAN

One of the primary functions of a template is to simply help you organize your thoughts. That alone can save you a lot of valuable time. I highly recommend you don't start a plan from scratch. Use templates and examples. Make it your own and modify accordingly, or use it as is, but start with a template.

As previously mentioned, I have been involved in strategic planning that resulted in massive amounts of documentation, three-inch-thick binders, and inflated egos, but not results. I have since become a big fan of short strategic plans. As important as they are, they needn't be massive.

Table 3.1 shows my version of a one-page strategic plan template. It follows the ProCESS Strategy recommendation and is designed to help you quickly organize your thoughts and commit them to "paper," all part of the approach to business as ART.

TABLE 3.1. TEMPLATE FOR THE ONE-PAGE STRATEGIC PLAN.

STRATEGIC PLAN			
ORGANIZATION:		**DATE:**	**VERSION:** 1.0
VISION		**TODAY**	

GOALS			
PROFITABILITY	**CUSTOMER SATISFACTION**	**EMPLOYEE SATISFACTION**	**SOCIAL RESPONSIBILITY**
1. 2. 3.	1. 2. 3.	1. 2. 3.	1. 2. 3.

RANK	STRATEGIC OBJECTIVES	DUE BY	TODAY'S REALITY
	OBJECTIVE		**CORRESPONDING INDICATOR**
1.			
2.			
3.			
4.			
5.			

STRATEGIC INITIATIVES					
RANK	**INITIATIVE**	**SUPPORTS STRATEGIC OBJECTIVE #**	**OWNER**	**DUE BY**	**OBJECTIVES**
1.					1. Obj 1 2. Obj 2 3. Obj 3
2.					1. Obj 1 2. Obj 2 3. Obj 3
3.					1. Obj 1 2. Obj 2 3. Obj 3

■ **THE CHAPTER 3 WRAP**

In this chapter, we identified five myths about strategic planning as follows:

- A strategic plan can only exist at the organization or company level.
- A strategic plan must look out more than five years.
- A strategic plan is only good if it is several pages long.
- A strategic plan has a defined completion date.
- A strategic initiative is the same thing as a strategy.

We also discussed and gave examples for steps four through eight of the twelve-step approach to business as ART and went into some detail on the difference between strategic plans and strategic initiatives.

This chapter introduced the notion of a ProCESS Strategy because no business book worth its salt is complete without coining at least two terms and this is one of them. But, more importantly, a ProCESS Strategy has four cornerstones of focus:

- **Pro**fitability
- **C**ustomer satisfaction
- **E**mployee **s**atisfaction
- **S**ocial responsibility

Finally, we discussed the elements of a template for a one-page strategic plan as a means to help you quickly, efficiently organize your thoughts and document a strategy.

In the next chapter, we will get into the difference between strategic planning and strategic management as well as steps nine through twelve of the twelve-step process.

Before proceeding, please answer the following questions:

- Do you have a formal strategy? If so, do others know about and understand it?
- Do you understand the difference between a goal and an objective?
- Do you know the difference between an initiative and a strategy?

We close this chapter with another quote from Max McKeown's *The Strategy Book:* "A great strategy meeting is a meeting of minds."

FOUR

STRATEGIC MANAGEMENT

No battle plan ever survives contact with the enemy.
HELMUTH VON MOLTKE THE ELDER, 19TH-CENTURY
GERMAN FIELD MARSHAL WHO CREATED A MODERN
METHOD FOR DIRECTING ARMIES IN THE FIELD

Wikipedia defines strategic management like this: "Strategic management involves the formulation and implementation of the major goals and initiatives taken by a company's top management on behalf of owners, based on consideration of resources and an assessment of the internal and external environments in which the organization competes."

Huh? What? I swear to goodness some people just like to hear themselves talk and see how many big words they can put into one very long sentence that extends far beyond what is necessary in order to impress upon us their highly advanced level of smart-a-did-itty.

See? I can do it too, only with smaller, made-up words. But in all seriousness, that definition is a great example of why I wrote this book. Things are just complicated beyond necessity. Leaders of small and medium-sized businesses don't have time for lengthy definitions and complex processes.

I think of it this way: strategic management is the management of today's tasks with an eye on tomorrow's vision.

▪ DUST: THE DIFFERENCE BETWEEN STRATEGIC PLANNING AND STRATEGIC MANAGEMENT

As said, it has been my experience that a majority of small to medium-sized businesses do not have formal strategic plans, and a lot of those that do, regardless of business size, don't do them well. Many waste their time with big, meaningless volumes of documents and then fail to proceed to the stages where they are actually executing or managing according to the plan. Quite literally, "dust" is the difference between even a good strategic plan and strategic management, because without the execution phase, that's all the plan is good for... gathering dust.

Home Depot has a great marketing slogan in which they close commercial spots with "More doing," and that's what we are really talking about when it comes to strategic management. At some point, you have to stop planning to redesign the bathroom and get to the task of doing it.

Strategic management encompasses steps nine through twelve of the twelve-step Business Is ART process, repeated here for your convenience (you're welcome):

9. Determine how you will manage the initiatives (project planning) and measure progress toward the completion of those initiatives.
10. Determine how you will manage the business itself.
11. Execute the plans and regularly measure your progress.
12. Continue to review, assess, refine, and modify the previous steps as necessary.

Chapter 6 of this book is dedicated to business planning, which is really what step ten is all about. Thereafter, the remainder of the book is all about steps eleven and twelve, which are rooted in tracking and reporting on objectives. Objectives are often communicated in the form of key performance indicators or KPIS, and even more simply as "metrics." In chapter 9, we introduce a new method for tracking and reporting metrics called the "Ping Chart." More on that later, but first, let's discuss strategic management and step nine in a bit more detail.

■ TASK MANAGEMENT VERSUS STRATEGIC MANAGEMENT

All men can see these tactics whereby
I conquer, but what none can see is the strategy
out of which victory is evolved.
SUN TZU, AUTHOR OF *THE ART OF WAR*

Wikipedia defines task management this way: "Task management is the process of managing a task through its life cycle. It involves planning, testing, tracking and reporting."[1]

Now that's a definition I can get behind, and if you consider my definition of strategic management, in conjunction with this definition of task management, you can see that strategic management is not just about managing the strategic plan. It is a way of conducting business every day in a way that is based in ART. You have to start doing something in order to have something to measure (Track), in order to know how effective your plans are, adjusting accordingly (Revise), and to restate what it is you are trying to do (Articulate).

A strategic plan is not tactical by nature, but strategic management can be. As the quote at the beginning of this chapter says, no plan survives initial contact with the enemy, and that is where the importance of tactics comes into play. You have to act and adjust tactically, but that doesn't mean you have to abandon the strategy.

For example, in our $50 million quest, part of our strategy was to build a certain service at our home office location because labor and leased space were less expensive than on the East Coast. But we quickly ran into a problem. Our growth outpaced the available pool of qualified employee candidates. So we changed tactics and identified a shortfall, then modified our plan to

---

1 Wikipedia contributors, "Task management," *Wikipedia, The Free Encyclopedia,* http://en.wikipedia.org/w/index.php?title=Task_management &oldid=654462326 (accessed April 2, 2015).

establish a small satellite office in a location on the East Coast that was expensive but was close to qualified and experienced resources. Our strategy still included disrupting the market, becoming a leader, and making the home office the primary delivery hub, but our tactics for hiring the best staff necessarily changed to include resources at another location.

We then went further and changed our sales tactics: we now boasted about having an additional facility that provided business continuity in the event of a disaster at the home office, turning what at first seemed like an added expense into a smart business approach and sales advantage.

From time to time, emergencies will come up that make you just say, "To hell with the vision and strategy: I have to survive this day." But if you find yourself saying that every day, chances are you are not managing strategically, you are only managing tactically.

■ DETERMINE HOW YOU WILL MANAGE STRATEGIC INITIATIVES

As previously mentioned, strategic initiatives are merely projects with strategic intent, but a key word is "project." Projects have defined start and end dates and clearly defined objectives.

There are many project management methodologies out there available to you. Most are consistent with the Project Management Body of Knowledge (PMBOK). PMBOK was designed by the Project Management Institute (PMI). The intent of this book is not to teach this project management methodology, or to create yet another one, but rather to introduce you to a few topics on project management. What methodology or tools you use are up to you, so long as you use something, and usually, something with a basis in PMBOK is your best bet. So let's spend a little time talking about PMBOK—probably more than you'd like, but stay with me because there is a point to it.

Project managers often seek to become certified project management professionals (PMPs). This is a very formal certification. You must have a certain level of experience to qualify, and then you study, receive training, take an exam, and pay fees. It is not for the faint of heart.

PMBOK defines five process groups (initiating, planning, executing, monitoring and controlling, and closing) plus ten knowledge areas, from project integration management to project stakeholder management. A PMP hopeful must become expert in each of these areas.

Now that we have spent a little time on this PMBOK, let me tell you something that is sure to enrage PMP certified project managers everywhere. You probably don't need it.

All right, all right, everybody. Just cool your jets for a minute and let me explain. In some lines of work, PMP certification is required, and if you want to become a better project manager, you will certainly learn a lot from becoming PMP certified. But for most small to medium-sized businesses and organizations, applying the full PMBOK to your project management methodology is like driving a two-inch nail with a sledgehammer. It might make you feel like a he-man, but it results in a poor outcome.

PMBOK covers a lot of territory that is great if you are building a spacecraft, but doesn't apply if you are determining how to improve customer satisfaction by baking them a tastier chocolate cake.

Few things are more frustrating than being forced to follow processes that do not appear to make sense. Anyone who has ever spent time around children is all too familiar with the famous question, "Why?" As leaders (and parents), all we want to say and all we want them to accept is, "Because I said so."

Indeed, sometimes, as a leader, that's precisely what you should demand. But only when there is no time for the question. Generally, leaders should only play that card when it is absolutely necessary, and when immediate, unquestioned action is the only way to survive the moment. Only fear or trust can give a leader that power, and I personally prefer trust. "I'm asking you to trust me this time and do it because I said so."

But as intelligent human beings, we should ask ourselves, "Why?" Why am I doing this? What is the value proposition? What is there to gain from doing this?

If in business you find yourself doing something simply because it's how it's always been done, or because a coach or consultant suggested it, but you honestly cannot point to any good reason or result: stop doing it.

Here is a fictitious conversation for illustrative purposes:

Business owner: I have a web site.

Consultant: That's great.

Business owner: I spend thousands of dollars a year on it.

Consultant: What kind of business does it generate for you?

Business owner: None. But my friends tell me it looks nice.

Consultant: Stop spending your money.

Now, in this example, I'm not suggesting the business owner should stop having a web site. I'm suggesting the business owner stop spending money on a web site or design that does not positively impact the bottom line, and start spending that money on one that does.

You should have a similar conversation with yourself when it comes to following any methodology or process. Does this particular process add value (or avoid risk, which is a value)? If not, don't do it. Always use caution and common sense when deciding what methodology or tools to use to manage your projects and initiatives.

■ THE BASIC COMPONENTS OF A PROJECT PLAN

To manage your projects and initiatives properly, the following basic components should be in your project plan:

- **The owner.** Who owns the plan and manages the project? This doesn't mean the person who does everything, but it is the person who makes sure everything gets done.
- **The goals and objectives.** We have already spent time discussing goals and objectives, but to reiterate: every strategic initiative and every project should have defined goals and objectives. Otherwise, we are just defining stuff to do that makes us feel better.
- **A schedule.** What needs to be done, by when, and how is it dependent on tasks that come before it?

Many people confuse the schedule with the plan. It isn't the plan. It is a component of the plan that tells you when things need to start and conclude, as well as what their dependencies are.

· **Resource assignments.** If you have an otherwise great plan but have failed to define the roles necessary and assign specific people to fulfill those roles, you just created a nice theory with no means to make it reality. As I write this, I am reminded of a scene from the movie *Michael*, in which John Travolta plays the archangel Michael. Michael says, "That was right around the time I invented standing in line... before that everybody just gathered around. It was all a big mess, so I said why don't we just make a line?" That's what a plan without assigned resources is like. Everybody just gathers around, waiting for something to happen.

· **Risk management plan.** We often ask, "What are the risks?" and stop there. Sometimes we stop because stating the risks out loud just scares the crap out of us. Sometimes we say, "Risks be damned" and forge ahead with the plan without going further in determining how to manage the risks. At a minimum, a risk management plan should include the following:

> Identification of the risk
> Likelihood that the risk will occur (percentage or odds)
> Impact its occurrence will have (small, medium, large)
> How you will mitigate the risk (work to avoid it or minimize its impact)

Identifying the mitigation approach is critical because it not only helps you determine your course of action, it also provides you with confidence (sometimes it's all about attitude). You may be going into something knowing there is risk involved, but at least it is calculated risk.

- **Communication plan.** In my experience, the number one critical piece of feedback that comes from employee satisfaction surveys, year after year after year is, "We need better communication." It's true in our everyday management of an organization, it's true of our vision and strategy, and it's certainly true in our projects and initiatives. Determine in advance what is to be communicated, via what media, by whom, to whom, and how frequently. A lot of projects become "black holes" because we fail to determine how we want aspects of the project to be communicated.

- **Determine a reward structure.** Unless you have deep pockets and money to burn, your strategic initiatives are going to require your employees to do things above and beyond their normal jobs, which often means working extra hours. Before you assign resources to the plan, determine how you are going to reward them for being a part of it. "Your reward is that I will be able to put more cash in my own pocket" is probably not a good strategy. It doesn't have to be a big reward, and it doesn't necessarily have to be cash, but determine ahead of time how you plan to reward your employees and communicate that to them before the project starts.

· **Determine how you will celebrate success.** Again, before the project starts, determine how you will celebrate its success. Envision the day the project is successfully completed. The celebration shouldn't necessarily be limited to the people who played a role in the project. If it's a strategic initiative, theoretically, anyone left standing afterward should benefit from the results, so it should be a cause for everyone within the organization to celebrate.

■ A WORD ON DELEGATING

You will launch many projects, but have time to finish only a few. So think, plan, develop, launch, and tap good people to be responsible. Give them authority and hold them accountable. Trying to do too much yourself creates a bottleneck.

DONALD RUMSFELD, FORMER

UNITED STATES SECRETARY OF DEFENSE

Raise your hand if you ever have been, or have worked for, someone who complains about being overworked but who insists on doing everything, being in every meeting, and delegating to no one? One of the worst work experiences of my professional life was when I reported to someone who did exactly that. I'd successfully led a complex, growing, profitable organization long before this person came along. Our styles were dramatically different except that we were both stubborn. We might have actually gotten beyond that point except that this person seemingly trusted no one. I'll never know whether that was because she honestly believed she was better than everyone else, or if at some point in her life someone had severely betrayed her trust, scarring her. I might have tried harder to find out if I hadn't witnessed her verbal and emotional abuse of nearly everyone within her domain.

That aside, what really made me miserable was that I could no longer do my job…a job that up until that point had made my team, my employees, and me thrive. On so many occasions I wanted to say, "If you are going to do my job for me, what do you need me for?" but I was too afraid her response would be, "You're right. I don't need you. You're fired," just out of spite. In hindsight, I really should have said it and let the chips fall where they might.

When you do not trust your team to get things done, you are insulting them and indirectly saying, "You aren't good enough."

But just as bad, if you are doing everything yourself, you are doing yourself and the organization a tremendous disservice on at least three fronts:

1. It doesn't matter if no one else can do it as well as you. So what if you can do it twice as fast as anyone on your team? Your most critical role is to lead the team—emphasis on lead. If you are mired in the muck of doing the everyday tasks with which your team should be entrusted, then you aren't focused on leading, and your business will suffer. If you don't trust the team to get it done, whose fault is that? Hint: yours.

2. The best way to learn is by doing. If your team truly isn't up to the task at hand, but appears otherwise

capable, they aren't going to be any more prepared the next time if you insist on continuing to do it yourself. At some point, for the sake of the future, you have to say, "It's your turn at the wheel." Don't put them in the driver's seat for the first time, send them onto the highway during rush hour, and say, "Good luck! Call me when you get there!" Teach them. Guide them. I honestly believe my former boss didn't want anyone else doing anything for fear they'd do it better than her, or for fear that someone higher up would notice one of her direct employees doing something better than she did. And that is a horrible way to lead. Conversely, employees should never try to one-up the boss or go around the boss's back. My first boss out of college taught me that the best way to look good is to make the boss look good. That might not sit well with some, but it is totally true. Do great work, make the boss look good, and you too will look good because in most cases, that boss is going to sing your praises...right after someone has sung theirs. For the boss to be scared that one of their employees will look great is idiotic. When the team looks great, the boss looks great. A boss who tries to do it all or take all the credit looks silly.

3. If you try to do everything yourself, something is going to fail somewhere: your business, your health, your personal relationships. Something. Will. Fail. It's just a matter of when and how bad. If for no other reason, delegate to give yourself a break.

■ STRATEGIC MANAGEMENT OF CUSTOMERS

Have you ever heard the expression "Business would be great if it weren't for the customers"?

I've actually worked with executives who seem to truly have that attitude, as if their company was doing its customers a tremendous service by permitting them to spend their money and place their trust in this business.

Strategically managing customers is not just providing them with a quality product at a reasonable price and reasonable payment terms. The strategic management of customers involves keeping them engaged after the initial sale. Depending on the type of customers you have for the type of business you run, involvement after the initial sale can take on many forms. Here are just a few:

- Assign an account manager. I briefly worked with a company that had client accounts ranging from a few thousand dollars a month to multiple millions in service revenue per year. Not a single account had an assigned account manager. The clients felt unappreciated. The employees felt they had multiple taskmasters, coordinating with the client on various issues, but rarely coordinating in-house with one another. The right hand almost never knew what the left was doing. Not one person had across-the-board institutional knowledge of the client, so when the contract came up for automatic and mandatory rebid, the effort to put together a winning proposal was made exponentially more challenging. Finding good, referenceable experiences to weave into the proposal proved nearly impossible. Questions as basic as "How is the project team performing against benchmarks?" were effectively met with the response, "What's a benchmark?" In looking at the client's history, there was a dramatic drop in the client's business at a particular point in time that otherwise didn't seem related to market conditions. Mind you, this was a business that the servicing company managed on behalf of the client. When I asked the servicing company what caused the dip, the response was, "I've no idea." An account manager should know everything there is to know about the clients, not just to provide more efficient support, but to anticipate their needs and therefore upsell to them. In this case, one person should be made responsible so that everyone in the company knows who to keep informed about the client.

· Send regular information. The key here is information. Provide clients with something they can use or tuck away in their knowledge bank. Establish yourself as the expert in whatever it is you're selling, no matter how big or small. Perpetuate that notion long after the initial sale by continually educating the customer.

· Consider sending regular newsletters. It seems these days everyone is sending newsletters, but most of them go in the trash. Why? Because most newsletters are either boldly, directly trying to sell you something, or are telling you a bunch of junk you do not care about. Find out what your target market cares about and then talk about it in an informative way. Make your newsletter visually appealing, grammatically accurate, and interesting. When the time comes, your readers will come to you for service. It's an investment with long-range payoffs, not something that brings immediate new sales.

· Send handwritten thank-you cards after the sale.

· Offer discounts for repeat customers. They don't have to be deep discounts, just a little something to say, "Hey, I appreciate your business."

· Occasionally do something for free, particularly when you know your customer is in a pinch. This runs counter to what a pure capitalist might think. The general school of thought is, "When they really need us the most, that's when we maximize the price." But that is really a tactical, not strategic, way to view things. It might work once, maybe even twice. But unless your business holds a monopoly over the market, that's it. They won't be back a third time.

This isn't by any stretch meant to be an exhaustive list, but hopefully it gives you a few things to think about in your strategic management.

And if none of this is news to you, perhaps at least it will make you think, "I know all of this. Maybe it's time I actually did something about it."

Why is it so important to strategically manage the customers? Because the best way to grow a business is by forming and maintaining a solid base. If you find yourself in a place where continuing to sell to the base of customers becomes comparatively easy, that frees up resources to focus on bringing in the next new customer. If you are constantly fighting to maintain a base, there simply is no time and resources for growth.

But just as importantly, establishing a good base of customers creates the best sales force you could have. If they are happy, they will recommend you to others. So never think of customers from a tactical point of view. Manage them strategically to ensure long-term revenue and growth.

■ AVOID THE BIG LIE

Whatever you do with respect to strategic management of your business, your employees, and your customers, avoid the "big lie" of insincerity. Saying things just because you think they are what someone wants to hear, or to avoid looking bad is tactical management, not strategic management. It cannot be sustained over the long haul.

Continuing with the $50 million example in this book, very early on, we recognized how important our base was to the feasibility of our $50 million objective. Without a steady base, we simply had no reasonable path to $50 million. Initially, we made a bold statement that we would lose no current customers. Later, we added "unless we want to" to that mantra. In chapter 6, we will discuss the need to sometimes fire a customer, but how did we maintain the ones we already had?

For starters, in our particular industries, it was the norm for potential clients to ask for at least three referenceable accounts for which we had performed similar work. So simply by the nature of our business, we had to strategically manage clients to maximize the formal references without which we could kiss further growth goodbye.

These are the two things we never wanted potential clients to hear from existing clients:

1. Well, we're kind of stuck with them now, but if we had to do it over again, we'd go with someone else.
2. Do not, I repeat, *do not* contract with these bozos!

We needed our clients to sing our praises. Sometimes that meant going the extra mile and even temporarily sacrificing a little margin. But we always counted on the payoff to come. For example, whenever there were enhancements that could be made to the software solutions we provided (that ultimately enabled our business process services), we had basically three choices: 1) do it only if someone was willing to pay for it, 2) do it at our own expense, or 3) don't do it.

It's always ideal if you can get a client to pay for an enhancement, and sometimes they do. But in this case, they would be paying for enhancements that would ultimately benefit us more than them. So it seemed to us that the better solution was to occasionally squeeze a little bit of our profit margins to "fund" enhancements (strategic initiatives), knowing that in the end, they would more than pay for themselves in internal efficiency gains, goodwill, a solid base of happy customers, and growth through reputation and referrals.

We also made the decision to always have a designated account manager, and sometimes a deputy account manager if the account was large enough to support the additional resource. We have already discussed the importance of this, so I won't go into further detail here. However, I feel it's worth sharing that the team that eventually acquired us thought this was over-kill and a waste of money, and they ended the practice. Not surprisingly, we began losing clients soon after. This was a classic case of not managing strategically. There was more interest in short-term gains than long-term sustainability.

A lot of our clients were government agencies, and there are very strict rules governing gifts or perceived gifts when dealing with the government. For those clients, we made a point of sponsoring lunch or a cookie break at industry conferences, and to have booths at these events. Again, our expectation was not to correlate sponsorship and attendance at their conferences to any one particular closed deal. Rather, it was our way of saying, "Thank you; we are invested in this with you."

This too became something we could no longer do once we were acquired. In our new world, conferences and trade shows were viewed solely as sales opportunities. If you couldn't come home from an industry conference with three qualified leads, the expense of attending or sponsoring could not be justified in the new company's eyes. And so, again, soon after we stopped being a sponsor, having a booth, or being well represented at industry conferences, we began to lose clients to those companies that were willing and able to be there.

We also held client appreciation functions for those clients who were able to accept. These were not sales meetings, these were truly appreciation functions. I would stand up for two minutes in front of the crowd to thank them for their partnership and share a couple of plans we had for the future, and then we would invite them to enjoy the food, drink, and music. That was it.

At the very first of these events we held after the acquisition, I was forced to give a fifteen-minute pitch to the attendees while their food grew cold back in the kitchen. It was an embarrassment; I felt like a timeshare salesman who had just snared a bunch of unsuspecting tourists into my sales presentation.

So the message is to be sincere in whatever you do to strategically manage the client relationship and build the base. These are smart people you are dealing with. They know a smoke screen when they see it. They know greed when they smell it.

■ THE CHAPTER 4 WRAP

In this chapter we discussed strategic management and briefly defined it as the management of today's tasks with an eye on tomorrow's vision. If you are managing in a way that destroys the potential to reach that vision, either you have the wrong vision, or you are managing solely for today, exchanging short-term gains for long-term sustainability. By default, strategic management starts with a strategic plan that includes identified initiatives.

A key to successful strategic management is to determine how you will manage. What methodologies and tools will you use? The best and most popular project management methodologies are based on the Project Management Institute's Project Management Body of Knowledge (PMBOK). But attempting to apply all that

PMBOK has to offer is usually overkill and can put you into a cycle of completing process for process's sake.

There are a few basic elements of a solid project plan that include but are not necessarily limited to the following:

- An assigned owner
- Clearly defined goals and objectives
- A schedule
- Defined roles and assigned resources
- A risk management plan
- A communication plan
- Defined rewards
- Celebration of success

Some of the success factors critical to strategic management include your willingness to delegate to others and how you strategically manage clients. Whatever you do, above all, be sincere in your actions; otherwise, customers and employees alike will recognize your insincerity, ultimately taking their skills and business elsewhere.

Before proceeding, please answer the following questions:

1. Do you know the difference between strategic planning and strategic management?
2. Would you say your management style is more tactical or more strategic?
3. Can you think of some examples?

FIVE

BEHAVIOR MANAGEMENT

Human behavior flows from three main sources:
desire, emotion, and knowledge.

PLATO

THE IMPORTANCE OF THIS TOPIC

This book discusses behavior management as it directly relates to approaching business as ART. It is not intended to be the be-all and end-all on the subject of behavior management. But the topic is important enough to dedicate an entire chapter to it.

Behavior management is so critical to a successful strategy and so often overlooked that I am putting very heavy emphasis on it, and I encourage you to seek out books, seminars, training, and consultants who specialize in it.

One such book is *The Behavior Breakthrough* by Steve Jacobs and colleagues. This book provides numerous examples and cites a multitude of other resources that you may look up for additional information.

To paraphrase something Jacobs says, the best strategy in the world can't succeed if those required to execute the strategy behave in ways that don't support the strategy.

Study the subject of behavior management and make it an important part of your operation and management philosophy. Keep it in the forefront of your mind every day.

Behavior management is often misunderstood. Some people think it is behavior manipulation. Others think it can only be handled by compensation. Still others think it is unnecessary (pay people to do their jobs and they do their jobs). You see behavior management often addressed formally in the education field, particularly in early childhood education, but it is more difficult to find sources of information on behavior management in the workspace.

A good way to think of behavior management is as the prevention of certain behaviors, such as sexual harassment, and the empowerment of people to manage their own behavior.

First, preventing certain behaviors. This book and this chapter are not intended to be a human resources how-to. But if you employ two or more people and are too small to have a human resources or legal department, it is crucial that you consult outside experts to, at a minimum, establish an employee handbook that defines the behaviors expressly not permitted in your place of business. Do not try to do this on your own, because the employment laws are complex and always changing. The types of behaviors we are talking about here are general conduct for legal, protective, and workplace culture purposes.

But there are performance-related behaviors you want to prevent as well. Perhaps a better way to think of it is that there are performance-related behaviors you want to enable. One way to enable these behaviors is to empower employees to manage themselves (so that you don't have to) in ways that support your vision and strategy.

That is the focus of the remainder of this chapter.

■ BEHAVIOR MANAGEMENT STARTS WITH YOU

Leadership is a matter of having people look at you and gain confidence, seeing how you react. If you're in control, they're in control.

TOM LANDRY, LEGENDARY NFL COACH

As an experiment, after reading Jacob's book *The Behavior Breakthrough*, I started a discussion thread on LinkedIn. I wanted to see how well people understood the concept of behavior management.

The discussion thread essentially started out like this: "Here is a hypothetical situation. You have an otherwise perfect strategy. The team understands the goals and objectives and believes them to be reasonable, but no progress is being made. How do you manage team behavior to support and execute the strategy?"

The responses were varied and many, but here is a rundown of the most common:

- Jon (you idiot), no strategy is perfect, so you started with a false assumption.
- If no one is executing the strategy, then it wasn't perfect (you fool).
- I'm an author on strategy. Buy my book (sucker).
- I'm a consultant. Contact me for help (chump).

I repeatedly restated the words "hypothetical" and "otherwise perfect" in follow-up responses. I even went so far as to say, "Forget about everything else for a minute... how do I get the behavior I want?"

To be fair, a couple of people got it—one of them was a retired military general. Otherwise, everyone else completely missed the point: how do you manage behavior?

Like so many other things in business and in life, there is no one right answer. That said, one golden rule is that your behavior management strategy starts with you. As a leader, you are on display at all times. How you behave sets the tone for your business or organization. This seems to go without saying, and yet, so many of us lose sight of it.

This goes both for general behavior and for momentary or spontaneous behavior. If you are constantly behaving in an angry way, you breed anger. If you are constantly goofing around, that breeds goofy behavior. Be aware at all times of how others are reading you. Every second of every work day, your employees are reading you.

One day, I came into the office after having a significant disagreement with a family member. I reacted poorly to the emotion of hurt and anger that I was feeling and let the disagreement influence my workplace behavior.

When I got into the office, instead of greeting people in my usual friendly way, I entered the break room with a scowl on my face, not looking at or engaging with anyone. I simply poured a cup of coffee and hurried back to my desk.

Later, one of the most trusted members of my leadership team knocked on my door and suggested that we needed to talk in private.

He closed the door and asked in a very concerned tone, "Are we going to announce layoffs?"

The question stunned me. We were growing. We were profitable. We had a couple of small layoffs early on in our path to $50 million, but that was part of the plan. I didn't know where the concern was coming from.

"No. Why?"

"There's a rumor going around."

"How did *that* get started?"

"Some employees were in the break room this morning and said you wouldn't even look them in the eye, so they started speculating about what was wrong. Then they concluded you couldn't look them in the eye because you are going to lay some of them off."

I started the rumor. Not knowingly or intentionally, but because I was not paying attention to my own behavior. This led employees to speculate about what was causing my "unnatural" behavior, and they "naturally" concluded I was about to chop some heads, starting with people lounging around the break room.

The good news was we dramatically cut back on the cost of coffee that day. But the bad news was we lost a lot of productivity to gossip and worry. Worse, I lost at least some of the faith and trust of some of my employees.

■ AFTER YOU, BEHAVIOR MANAGEMENT STARTS WITH COMMON COURTESY

*If we accept being talked to any kind of a way,
then we are telling ourselves we are not quite
worth the best. And if we have the effrontery to talk
to anybody with less than courtesy, we tell ourselves
and the world we are not very intelligent.*
MAYA ANGELOU, AUTHOR AND POET

There have been a number of tools that I have employed to influence and manage behavior over the years, including: humor, a strong work ethic, appealing to civic and moral obligation, formal incentive and recognition programs, and informal programs and events.

There is no one-size-fits-all approach. Everyone is motivated differently, but my personal opinion is that common courtesy is at the heart of behavior management. If you foster an environment in which courtesy is encouraged, expected, and displayed, it makes all other aspects of behavior management easier.

For example, if you see someone at the grocery store who needs a little help getting their bags in the car, you might stop and lend a hand. This is a win-win for both of you. Just think how much more efficient and productive things would be at work if everyone behaved this way. Smile and say "hello" when passing one another in the halls or on the floor. Give someone a genuine pat on the back and say, "Nice job" or, "How's it going?" more often. Offer to help someone who is struggling, even though it isn't part of your job description.

Just saying the words, "Here, let me help you with that," creates good will. Make common courtesy contagious, and bigger things will follow.

One of many tactics I used was to write a monthly newsletter and publish it on an internal web site. The page included monthly shout-outs to employees who had achieved something significant that month, or who had received e-mails or letters from clients singing their praises. For this newsletter, I also wrote an article each month. Usually, it made some point about workplace behaviors, but sometimes it was just to educate or to get people to think about something.

Continuing with the coffee and break-room theme, see the sidebar below, "Please Make a New Pot of Coffee," for one such article that received a lot of employee feedback and created a very positive buzz up and down the halls. While the story itself might not directly relate to employee behavior, at the end of it all, it was about encouraging common courtesy.

PLEASE MAKE A NEW POT OF COFFEE—COMMON COURTESY

One of my workplace pet peeves is to walk into the break room and find that no one has made coffee. This is true whether I am actually going for a cup or not. It is just simple common courtesy to make more if the office coffee pot is running low or empty.

It is a fairly simple process to make a pot of coffee. And it communicates something very important. Along this principle, let me tell you a story about a trip I recently took with my seventy-year-old father. A series of health issues over the last eight years have left Dad in a wheelchair and with severe chronic pain. Despite it all, he does his best to get around and live as normally as possible. But it is difficult in a world that is not designed for "people like him."

During our trip, which included air travel, we always took advantage of being able to board first, and we sat in the front row so that Dad would not have far to go to get from the wheelchair at the plane's doorway to the seat. Each time, people gave me dirty looks for boarding first with him. On the final leg of our trip home, Dad and I waited for his chair to arrive, sitting patiently while others hurried off the plane. When his chair was ready, he got up to get his bag down from the overhead storage, despite my insistence that I would get it for him.

Unfortunately, someone had placed a larger bag on top of Dad's, and he was struggling to get his down. He was probably in the aisle for all of five seconds, but a well-dressed man decided he could not wait the remaining few seconds it would have taken Dad to get his bag down. He shoved Dad aside and exited the plane.

One of the airline employees saw what happened and kindly offered to carry Dad's bag and push him all the way out to the parking garage. We took him up on the offer only as far as to baggage claim, and I handed him a tip for his efforts. And there, sure enough, pacing aimlessly and without regard to anyone else, texting on his BlackBerry, was the same man who had shoved Dad aside.

Dad rolled up to him, got his attention, and said, "I just want you to know I really appreciate you shoving me like that."

The man looked at Dad with absolute disgust, grunted and walked away.

As loudly as I could without shouting, I said, "I guess he doesn't care what you appreciate," and Dad and I shared an uncomfortable laugh about it.

After we got our bags, Dad rolled out to the passenger pickup area while I went to bring the car around.

While I was gone, the same man left the airport in the same spot as my Dad, and without making eye contact, as he passed Dad, he said, "Take a shower next time you travel."

Because of his physical condition, Dad is unable to take a shower. But every morning and every night, he gives himself a sponge bath. It hurts his pride greatly to only be able to bathe this way, but he does it religiously. That he had in fact not taken a shower was something the man could not possibly have known, and Dad's personal hygiene was not really at issue. The man was merely making a childish statement to get "even" with Dad for embarrassing him.

Dad's response to the man is not something I can print here. Had I been there, I don't know what my response would have been.

I like to think that the man is just a pompous jerk. I also like to think he is in the extreme minority. I like to believe most people are, generally speaking, courteous and kind. And if we are not, we should be.

All that man had to do was say, "I am sorry about that," and everything would have been all right.

Please remember to choose your words and your actions wisely. Show some common courtesy. Remember your manners. Something that may not cause you to bat an eye could ruin someone else's day.

In closing, remembering my own manners, in advance, I thank you for your cooperation when I say, "Please make a new pot of coffee."

Always remember that behavior management starts with you, but it goes way beyond how you behave, as important as that is. Behavior management is about how you purposefully, thoughtfully, and systematically influence behavior, and at the heart of that is fostering an environment that promotes and expects common courtesy.

Now, let's break down and discuss the quote by Plato that opened this chapter.

■ THE THREE PILLARS OF BEHAVIOR MANAGEMENT

Desire, emotion, and knowledge are the three pillars of behavior management. As previously mentioned, an otherwise great strategy that doesn't address behavior management will produce poor results, or at best, not maximize results. My opinion is that most people in the workforce want to do a good job that they can be proud of. Most employers want exceptional performance from their employees. If this is true, then there is already a possibility of a chasm. What is "good enough" in the employee's mind may not be good enough in the employer's mind. So how do you bridge the gap?

Start by considering the three pillars and ask yourself three basic questions:

1. What does the employee desire?
2. What gets the employee to feel a positive emotion about the job and the company?
3. What does the employee know?

A big part of ART is being flexible and wise enough to make revisions to plans, and the same is true of our assumptions. You have to be flexible and wise enough to revise them. Never presume or assume you know the answers to the questions we just posed. Take time to discover them. This is actually a key difference between consulting and contracting. A contractor knows what the client wants because the client has specified it in the request for proposal. But the consultant must discover what the client needs by taking time to ask questions and listen to verbal and nonverbal clues. Once the consultant has a pretty good idea, they can assess whether or not there is something of value in their services for the client. If so, a proposal is developed.

If not, the honest consultant will say, "I'm sorry, but I can't help you."

It is the same thing when developing a behavior management strategy. Ask the questions. Seek the answers. Then determine if you can establish a strategy that will create the behaviors in your team that you want and need in order to accomplish your mission. If so, formalize the strategy.

If not, you may have some tough decisions to make. You might have to tell some employees, "I'm sorry, but I can't help you," which could mean any number of things from "I can't help you with this particular issue" to "You're fired."

In *The Behavior Breakthrough*, Steve Jacobs says, "New results require new behavior. It's that simple—and that difficult."[1]

Influencing new behavior is indeed a very difficult thing to do, but we have a much better shot at it if we understand the three pillars of behavior management. The following section breaks them down.

■ THE THREE PILLARS DEFINED

Let's define and discuss each of the three pillars of behavior management. The first is "desire."

Wikipedia defines desire as follows: "Desire is a sense of longing or hoping for a person, object, or outcome. The same sense is expressed by emotions such as 'craving' or 'hankering.' When a person desires something or someone, their sense of longing is excited by the enjoyment or the thought of the item or person, and they want to take actions to obtain their goal."[2]

Marketers have long used desire in advertising. The goal is to get people to want the product or service, or

---

1 Steve Jacobs and colleagues, *The Behavior Breakthrough* (Austin, Texas: Greenleaf Books, 2013).

2 Wikipedia contributors, "Desire," *Wikipedia, The Free Encyclopedia*, http://en.wikipedia.org/w/index.php?title=Desire&oldid=649555575 (accessed March 24, 2015).

to behave in certain ways by appealing to emotions that vary from fear to feeling good. The same is true of behavior management in the workplace. Let's look at a couple of examples.

When we developed the $50 million strategy, we painted a picture representing it and got people to understand it. Now we had to get them to want it. They had to desire it. In a way, we answered the question posed by one doubter, "Why would we ever want to do this?" by saying, "Because you are *that* good."

.We certainly believed that, but we also played very heavily to the notion that our services helped people who needed help. We put pictures of a financially struggling mother and her baby on the wall and said, "That's your *real* customer. Who can help her better than *you*?"

We played to the greed of competitors who focused on our markets simply because there was money to be made. We admitted to ourselves that, "Hey, we want to make money too, but there is something bigger than that here."

We made bold statements like, "We are taxpayers. We want to see these government programs be as efficient and effective as they can be because *we are paying for them*. Who better to deliver the services these programs need than us...than you? Who better to protect our tax money than ourselves?"

We made desire a very big component of our behavior management strategy in this way, and we could do it honestly and meaningfully. We didn't have to make stuff up; we just had to make it relatable and real.

Emotion is the second pillar and is closely related to desire.

Wikipedia defines emotion as follows: "In psychology and philosophy, emotion is a subjective, conscious experience characterized primarily by psychophysiological expressions, biological reactions, and mental states."[3] It also says that "Emotion...is often intertwined with mood, temperament, personality, disposition, and motivation. It also is influenced by hormones and neurotransmitters such as dopamine, noradrenaline, serotonin, oxytocin, cortisol and GABA.... Emotion is often the driving force behind motivation, positive or negative. An alternative definition of emotion is a 'positive or negative experience that is associated with a particular pattern of physiological activity.'"[4]

Many people talk about controlling your emotions. I would say that what we do is control how we behave in response to an emotion. I don't know how effectively one can really control emotions without the use of drugs, alcohol, or other chemicals. That said, I do subscribe to the school of thought that says that when you wake up in the morning, you can decide whether you're going to be in a good or bad mood. But mood and emotion aren't necessarily the same thing.

For example, suppose I have decided to will myself into a good mood. The day starts pretty well. I have a great cup of coffee, a healthy breakfast, and a nice hug and kiss from my lover. I'm probably even whistling and looking very nerdy. Then I step outside and right into

---

3   Wikipedia contributors, "Emotion," *Wikipedia, The Free Encyclopedia,* http://en.wikipedia.org/w/index.php?title=Emotion&oldid=650822661 (accessed March 24, 2015).

4   Ibid.

a pile of dog doo-doo left by the neighbor's pooch. My emotional response is probably not one of happiness. Aside from being grossed out, I'm probably a little mad.

At this point, one of several things could happen. I could take off my shoe and, playing to the emotion of anger, throw it at the first thing that moves. I could scream out loud about the thoughtless neighbor who let his dog poop in my yard without cleaning it up.

I could look to the sky and scream, "My God, why hast thou forsaken me?" or I could say, "Well, this sucks, but...doo-doo happens."

If I chose not to let the emotion ruin my otherwise good mood, I'd either clean my shoes or change them, get another kiss from my lover, and start whistling and looking nerdy again, not letting the emotion of anger alter my good mood.

If we can't control our own emotions, only our response to them, we certainly can't control the emotions of others. And likewise, we can certainly do things to influence emotions in others. The following are a couple of examples. Both are workplace related, but they're from very different situations.

There is a difference between mission and purpose. The "purpose statement" is what really puts emotion behind what it is you do. Although we wrongly called it our mission, our purpose was, "We help make the lives of those we serve just a little bit better." This was purely an emotional appeal to and bragging rights for our employees.

"I'm going to help these people in need, and I'm going to feel good about myself for doing it." That is very powerful and describes exactly the emotion we wanted the employees to feel.

In the second example, we had an employee who I will call "Joe" in one of our smaller satellite offices. Joe was highly compensated but rarely seen. When he was around, he was kind of cantankerous and disruptive, and he demonstrated an offensively high opinion of himself, which caused frequent complaints from others.

Even if none of those other things had been true, there would still have been one glaring thing staring me in the face: I had no idea what Joe did...and he worked for me. Once we had a vision and a plan in place, it became very clear that whatever this guy did, his work didn't support the plan, and neither did his behavior.

But we weren't cold, heartless jerks willing to swing the axe anytime something seemed amiss, so we took time to understand his role. It turned out that he really didn't do anything. When he was out of the office, he was supposedly meeting with a nearby large client, but we heard from the client that that was not the case. We gave him some specific functions to perform. We gave him some specific personal behavior improvements to make. We formalized all of this in a performance improvement plan. He ignored the plan; we fired him.

When the day came to let him go, my human resources director and I flew to the satellite office and arrived unannounced. We also wanted to talk to another employee at this office, who I will call "Bob," about a promotion. Bob was at the client site, and when we phoned him, he told us what time he'd be back. So we waited until Joe finally strolled in close to lunchtime.

I opened the subsequent meeting by saying, "Joe, we are here to inform you that your services are no longer required." Then I shut up while the human resources director proceeded with the next steps.

Infuriated, Joe told me what a piece of crap I was. He called me every name in the book.

As this was happening, all but one square inch of me was screaming, "Don't let him treat you like that!"

But the remaining one square inch said, "First, he is scared, hurt, and angry. Let him blow off steam. Second, letting him bait you into an argument or fight would open the doors to the possibility of being sued. Third, you did your homework and you know this had to be done. Fourth, the only person in the room whose behavior you can control is your own."

So, I maintained eye contact with him and did my best to hold an emotionless poker face. When Joe was done with his rant, he stared at me intently for a little bit. I stared back in silence.

Finally, he shook his head in disgust and said, "Sheeze," got up, and walked out.

Afterward, the human resources director told me that she'd seen things like that go sideways too many times, and my response to Joe's attack was exactly what I should have done.

Meanwhile, as Joe walked out of the building, Bob, whom we wanted to promote, had just pulled up. Joe proceeded to tell Bob that he himself had just been fired and we were there to fire Bob as well. We could see and hear the conversation just outside the door, but could do nothing about it.

So Bob came in literally shaking with anger, and probably fear. I extended a hand to greet Bob. A smile would have been false, but I did try to wear an expression that said "Relax," and the first words out of my mouth were, "Your employment isn't being terminated..."

I talked as much as I could without violating Joe's rights and confidentiality about our decision to let him go, then quickly moved onto our plans to promote Bob. We tied both decisions to the company's vision and strategy. We didn't speak poorly of Joe. We didn't leave Bob fearful he could be next, or feeling guilty for getting promoted while Joe was fired. And we didn't try to put on any false airs that everything was OK. But we wanted Bob to know he was important and had the talents to support the strategy and do the job.

As we did, we could slowly see his emotions going from fear and anger through understanding, to appreciation, and finally pride.

There are a couple of very solid lessons in the exchange with Bob. First, he showed enormous restraint himself because he saw how angry Joe was and heard from Joe what a rotten guy I was. Had he come in attacking me, I probably would have responded by at least not promoting him.

Second, because we controlled our own behavior and summoned the right emotions for the situation, it fostered a level of trust in Bob that resulted in his doing a pretty darned good job over the next few years. Without that, he might not have been as dedicated, loyal, and supportive of the strategy as he was.

How others choose to behave is completely out of our control, but it's a pretty good bet that if you nurture positive emotions in others, their behavioral response will in turn be positive.

Knowledge is the third pillar of behavior management.

Wikipedia defines knowledge as follows: "a familiarity, awareness or understanding of someone or something, such as facts, information, descriptions, or skills, which is acquired through experience or education by perceiving, discovering, or learning."[5]

From a behavioral perspective, it doesn't matter if we know something factually, or whether we just think we do. It's all the same. It induces some kind of behavioral response. From a risk and reward point of view, if we "know" we will never be appreciated for a job well done, or for going over and above expectations, then the long-term likelihood is that we will not do the job well or put in extra effort.

Using the example of Joe and Bob again, had Bob entered the room "knowing" that what Joe told him was true, his first words might have been "You sunny beach," or something like that. But he was wise enough to recognize that he didn't know anything and had the patience to learn for himself.

Conversely, if we know we will be recognized and perhaps rewarded, there is a better chance that we will do the job well or go beyond expectations. Note there

5 Wikipedia contributors, "Knowledge," *Wikipedia, The Free Encyclopedia,* http://en.wikipedia.org/w/index.php?title=Knowledge&oldid=653206343 (accessed March 24, 2015).

is a *better chance* of it. There is no guarantee, because, among other things, Plato's other two sources of behavior (desire and emotion) are at play.

A good behavioral management approach in the workplace recognizes these three sources of behavior and attempts to address each. Now let's discuss some myths about behavior management.

■ BEHAVIOR MANAGEMENT MYTHS

There are many myths about workplace behavior management. Some of the more common myths are the following:

1. Behavior management means monetary bonus plans.
2. Behavior management means that if you do your job, you won't get fired.
3. Behavior management means I only hire people who behave the way I want, and I fire those who don't.
4. Behavior management means everyone knows the vision, strategy, goals, and objectives of the company, and they'd damn well better get in line with them.
5. They got their bonuses and should be happy.

The sections that follow break down each of these myths.

Myth 1: Behavior Management Means Monetary Bonus Plans
This simply isn't true, yet bonus money is the first place our minds take us when we think of rewards. I do very much believe in monetary bonus plans, but the existence

of such a plan doesn't necessarily result in desired behavior, nor does reward necessarily mean "expense" or cost. There are many ways to reward employees that cost little to nothing. There are three concepts here we want to address: providing incentives for behavior, and a look at "expense" from two points of view.

First, a bonus plan doesn't necessarily result in desired behavior. If you have a bonus plan, it must be defined and formal. It is a contract between you and your employees. You review it, discuss it, and sign it together. But as you develop formal bonus plans, be sure that they reward the desired behavior. For example, one of my clients has a quarterly bonus plan that has one objective: to collect a certain amount of cash in the given quarter. That's it.

There are several things wrong with this plan. First, it is a small, ten-employee business. There are only two people in the office who directly affect cash receipts. They work the front desk and keep the books. The other eight people in the office are busy delivering the service that results in cash receipts. They influence cash receipts by doing good, quality work that keeps the customers coming back. They should have performance objectives of their own that maximize production at or above stated quality levels.

But if they only have incentives, above and beyond their normal pay, for cash receipts, they "know" two things:

1. They can't control how well the front desk collects payments, so their bonus is largely outside their control.

2. If they can influence it at all, it is by upselling unnecessary services to the client or rushing clients through in order to get to the next one more quickly.

In neither case is the bonus plan resulting in positive behavior. Worse, it causes behavior that ultimately results in lower client satisfaction, which in turn ultimately reduces cash receipts. The bonus plan creates exactly the opposite effect it was intended to have, not just on the behavior of the service team, but on the bottom line.

Adding fuel to the fire, the bonus plan does not reward the right behavior at the front desk either. While working with the client, we discovered that the accounts receivable was at a massively unacceptable level, with an alarmingly high amount more than ninety days overdue. Obviously, the bonus plan was not resulting in the desired behavior, and in that quarter, there was obviously no bonus paid.

But in the next quarter, staff made a large effort to collect past-due amounts. This was a lower-than-average quarter for sales, but thanks to the collection of past-due amounts, the team actually exceeded the quarterly objective. You see, it was not defined well enough to exclude past-due collections. There were probably two consecutive quarters in which the bonus target in collections from sales that quarter was not met. But because the accounts receivable had stacked up so high in the previous quarter, when it was collected in the next and in combination with that quarter's collections from sales, it resulted in a bonus payout.

For the record, I am not suggesting the front desk did this deliberately. But once it happened, what incentive did they have to never do it again? None.

Now let's look at things from the expense angle. As previously stated, a bonus plan does not necessarily mean expense, and there are two ways to look at this. The first is obvious, and everyone gets it right away. Some reward programs don't cost you anything. Every day, honest pats on the back should just be part of your operating model, but you can define other programs that formally recognize and reward employees that cost you little to nothing.

For example, you can award time off with pay. Everyone loves a day off or an extra vacation day. It costs you virtually nothing to do this. At worst, you or others might have to work a little harder on that day (or half day).

Another possibility is to define a multitiered recognition program that starts with employees nominating each other, based on objective criteria, to receive a peer recognition award. These can be nonmonetary "awards," such as a certificate and the employee's name going up on the wall. Tier two could have a $25 gift card associated with it. Tier three might have a more substantial monetary value, but this level is awarded less often and in the grand scheme of things still doesn't really cost much. The point is, there are all kinds of ways to reward employees without breaking the bank.

Finally, stop looking at bonus plans as an expense in the first place. Sure, you have to see it that way on the profit and loss statements, but make a mental shift. If your bonus plan is ultimately an expense—a true expense that negatively impacts your bottom line—then you have not designed it properly. Design your bonus plans to reward the right behavior that results in an increase in the top line and a decrease in overall expenses. When the bonus targets are achieved, the "expense" of the bonus is outweighed by the top and bottom line results.

I once worked for a company that had a bad experience paying a very large commission to a salesperson. In this case, the salesperson's incentive was based on the total contract value of the sale. So when he sold a $30 million deal, he couldn't care less that he had underbid the work by at least $10 million. He collected his check, bought a new car, and was very, very happy.

A year later, when the company realized it could not profitably deliver what it had promised, and that salesperson had moved on to another company, there was hell to pay for everyone. As a result, the company did two major things. First, it implemented a deal review process that included the salesperson, the project manager, finance, legal, and other executives. The review team could weed out bad deals before they occurred or improve proposals before they were delivered. This was all a good thing, even though it was painful for everyone involved, especially the salesperson.

But the second thing they did, which was not so smart in my opinion, was to change the sales commission plan. Actually, they did away with commissions and went to a straight bonus plan. This wasn't necessarily a bad move in and of itself, but it did bring problems. A commission is generally based on total contract value while a bonus plan is typically based on multiple objectives. The move to a bonus plan did drive away some of the hardcore and very good sales people. Earning commissions was their way of life, so they sought them elsewhere. But for those who stayed and those new to the company, there was a larger problem. The bonus plan for the salesperson was rebuilt around the profit achieved by the delivery team.

This created a number of issues. First, the salesperson has no direct control over the delivery team's performance, which directly affects profitability. Second, it made the salesperson focus backward on deals that had already been sold, instead of forward on deals in the pipeline.

The argument was that the company did not want to reward salespeople for bad deals. But that was exactly the point of the deal review board and process. By taking things a step beyond the deal reviews and tying the sales bonus to profit, the company caused salespeople to stop paying attention to selling more deals and to start paying attention to already sold deals. In this case, the bonus plan was very much an expense item.

Myth 2: Behavior Management Means That
If You Do Your Job, You Won't Get Fired
I've heard employers ask time and again why they should provide incentives for people to do their jobs, when a paycheck should be enough. Taking this attitude is a huge mistake, and here is why.

I believe that most people in the workforce desire to do a good job. Doing good, quality work produces an emotional response of feeling good, feeling proud, and feeling happy. We want to do good work.

The employer, however, wants us to do exceptional work. No one says, "I'll take a team of functioning average players any day over a team of functioning super-stars." (Note that the word "functioning" is included to keep things on an equal playing field, so don't give me no lip about superstars.)

From the start, there is a chasm in expectations because what we legitimately see as good work that makes us feel good may not be good enough for the employer. So it is very important to set expectations. Formally. Define "good enough" in your organization, and then stretch it a little bit to say, "This is exceptional."

Don't go crazy. Be realistic. Think about what most people, not you the rock star, can achieve in the course of a work day. Then add maybe 10 percent to that and say, "This is what I expect of you." What you are paying people a base salary for is the "good enough." You are providing incentives to go beyond "good enough" and achieve "exceptional performance," even if in your own mind exceptional is simply what you expect.

So the next time you catch yourself saying, "Why am I paying you if you can't even do your job?" ask yourself, "Did I properly define and communicate the expectations of this job?"

Myth 3: Behavior Management Means
I Only Hire Those People Who Will Behave
the Way I Want, and I Fire Those Who Don't
Wrong. First, hiring and firing costs real money, so you must not be cavalier about either of them. Granted, we don't intentionally hire people who we expect will not behave in the ways we want, unless we are bent on may-hem and destruction. But it is not uncommon at all to

fail to set expectations correctly, which can ultimately set the employee and you up for failure. This starts with the job posting, continues with the job description, goes further with the interview process, is reemphasized in greater detail in the new-hire orientation, and finally is spelled out clearly as performance objectives that are reviewed and signed off on by the manager and the employee.

If you fail to do this, you are very likely to hire someone who has no realistic shot at behaving in the ways that you want or need. But now that they are on board, and their behavior needs to change, what can you do?

Go back to the start. Have expectations been clearly and properly defined? Have they been effectively communicated? Beyond getting fired, are there any consequences for not meeting expectations? Have those been effectively communicated?

If the answer is always "no," then the misbehaving employee isn't the problem. You, Mr. or Ms. Rock Star, are the problem. Chances are pretty good in this scenario that all you are doing is complaining to whoever will listen that the employee is bringing you down.

But before you say, "You are so right, Jon. I need to fire that dude," let me encourage you to take a deep breath and ask yourself a few more questions.

Start with, "Does the employee know what the job is?" Be very candid with yourself or your managers about this. So often, we hire people that we think can do the job. We think they should know the job, or else why would they apply in the first place? They want to do a good job. They know the expectations and the consequences of not doing a good job. But do they know the job? There is a very good chance they do not, and there is a greater chance that is not their fault.

Next, do they know how to do the job? They might know the job itself, but doing it here may be different than what they were accustomed to elsewhere. You have to be certain that the employee both knows what the job is and knows how to do it. This sounds so simple and yet is so often assumed rather than ensured. In fact, a good rule of thumb is to assume that no new hire knows how to do the job. Likewise, assume no internal employee promoted to a new position knows how to do the job.

Finally, if you do all of this and still get nothing, there are two more questions to ask:

1. Is this person capable of doing what is expected?
2. If not, can I live with it?

If the answer to both of those questions is "no," then it is time to let that person go, or forever hold your peace about it because you only have yourself to blame. In that case, you are doing both yourself, and that employee a tremendous disservice. Worse, you are doing a disservice to those who are behaving within expectations. And worse yet, you are now giving everyone an incentive to behave below expectations.

The bottom line is that while people are responsible for their own behavior, we as employers are responsible for influencing the behavior we want or need by creating a culture that does the following:

- Ensures everyone knows and is capable of meeting the expectations
- Rewards people for behaving within or above expectations
- Doles out consequences for not behaving within expectations

Myth 4: Everyone Knows the Vision, Strategy,
Goals, and Objectives of the Company, and They'd
Damn Well Better Get in Line with Them
This is actually one of the main points of Business Is ART. If you take nothing else away from this book, take this: You must articulate the vision in understandable terms or no one else can get on board with it.

That said, you have to have painted the picture, set the goals and objectives, communicated the plans, and set expectations. If you have done all of this, not just once, but continuously, and someone just can't or won't get in line, fine. By all means, let them go. Their attitude can become a cancer within your organization. But you have to honestly assess whether you have done everything that you yourself should be doing before making that call.

If I had known who wrote the note "Why would we ever want to do that?" in response to my question "How can we get to $50 million?" I would have sought that person out and had a frank discussion about why they felt that way, then assessed whether I felt they could make it in our organization. I am fairly sure that they did not make it.

Myth 5: They Got Their Bonuses and Should Be Happy
Behavior management starts at the very top (at work or at home). However you define "incentive," be prepared to a) deliver on your promise in a timely manner and b) do it with obvious joy, pride, and appreciation.

I've seen leaders who pay bonuses reluctantly and grudgingly when employees meet or exceed the leader's own criteria, leaving employees feeling guilty or less than flattered for accepting what they earned. This in turn encourages the opposite behavior of that desired.

The subject of behavior management reminds me of a time when I would not have been eligible for "father of the year." My son, now an officer in the army, was eight or nine at the time and very badly wanted a Game Boy. But he'd been slacking a bit in school, so we made a deal. Get good grades on the next report card and get a Game Boy.

Several weeks later, he came home bouncing off the walls with excitement. He had received a fantastic report card. I momentarily got excited with him, hugged and high-fived him, told him "congratulations," and then went back to doing whatever unimportant thing I was doing.

He stood there for a moment, and then asked if I was ready to go. For what? To go get that Game Boy I'd promised.

I dismissed him as being somewhat ridiculous and continued doing whatever it was I was doing, telling him, "We'll go this weekend," making it obvious that I had more important things to do right then.

Over the next few minutes, it dawned on me that the look on his face had been heartbreaking, so I went up to his bedroom to find him crying softly. He wasn't mad at me. He was upset with himself. He felt stupid for thinking the promise was real. He felt greedy for wanting that Game Boy so badly. He felt guilty for so rudely interrupting Daddy, who was very busy with "important" stuff. Within moments, we were in the car headed to the store.

I learned a very valuable and painful lesson that day and have applied it ever since. Encouraging good behavior with the promise of a reward is a wonderful thing to do. But when that reward is earned, pay it immediately, joyfully, and in celebration. Being as excited and happy to give that award—perhaps even more so than the person receiving it—is significant.

■ BONUS AND PAY-FOR-PERFORMANCE PLANS

Behavioral leadership focuses on crafting
desirable shifts in everyday habits, behaviors, and routines.
STEVE JACOBS, *THE BEHAVIOR BREAKTHROUGH*

We have already discussed several dos, don'ts, and gotchas with respect to behavior management, and one of the things I keep coming back to is making absolutely certain that you are not the problem. You are the one responsible for crafting and influencing the everyday habits, behaviors, and routines of your employees.

One way to do this is to establish formal bonus plans and formal pay-for-performance plans that set expectations, influence the behavior you want, and make a positive impact on the bottom line (and hence should not be thought of as an expense). Bonus plans typically target the behavior of executives, managers, and leaders. Pay-for-performance plans typically target the behavior of the in-the-trenches, boots-on-the-ground employees. You know...the people who work for a living.

Some people see pay-for-performance as a specific type of bonus plan, but for the purposes of this book, I will discuss it separately. For our purposes, a bonus is something that is earned on top of base pay, and is typically dependent on organizational or company objectives being met in addition to individual performance. Bonuses are usually paid on a less frequent basis, such as quarterly, twice a year, or once a year.

By contrast, pay-for-performance is a variable component to a regular paycheck. There is a fixed component, plus a variable component that is based on individual and perhaps team production and quality objectives, but is paid with regularity.

In this next section, we will continue to discuss bonus plans. After that, we will discuss pay-for-performance plans.

Bonus Plans
A few things to keep in mind when determining bonus plans include:

1. Make it a formal contract.
2. Include only measurable objectives that tie directly to the business plan (or strategic plan depending on circumstances).
3. Make it realistic.
4. Make sure it rewards the right behavior.

I recommend that bonus plans have no more than three objectives. One of these objectives should be a company objective. A second should be a functional area or organizational objective. A third should be an objective tied specifically to the individual's performance. This approach helps ensure you are rewarding the desired behaviors at all levels.

I have seen bonus plans in which nothing at all is within the direct control of the bonus plan recipient. I have fallen victim to plans like this when I overachieved my targets, while others didn't meet theirs, so that no one received a bonus. This all-for-one and one-for-all approach generally does not work.

If Michael Jordan had received the same incentives as Dennis Rodman, would he have stuck around? He is probably one of the exceptions: one of those people who will perform beyond expectations regardless of reward because winning and being the best are what motivates and rewards them. But would he have done it in Los Angeles instead of Chicago? Possibly. Would it have been worth it to the Bulls to take that risk? Definitely not.

On the other hand, the "every man, woman, and child for themselves" approach is even more foolish and risky. If Jordan's compensation had been tied to his individual performance, would the Bulls have been as legendary as they were? Would he have been? Dennis Rodman, Scottie Pippen, and others were specialty and special players in their own right. They had crucial roles to play. If Jordan had tried to do it all simply for the sake of his own, individual stats, he would do so at the risk of losing games, losing championships, burning out, and getting injured.

The same holds true in business. A well-structured bonus plan that provides incentives for both outstanding individual and team efforts rewards the kind of behavior you want.

Once you have defined objectives in this manner, determine how much weight to give them. Are they all weighted equally? Does one have more or less weight than others? There is no one right answer. It may vary from year to year depending on your vision, strategy, and plans. Do what feels right for you and your organization.

As you do this, if you haven't already, determine how much the bonus plan will pay. One method for doing so is to work backward, following a simplified step-by-step method, or you can simply say "My bonus pool is X percent of my total salary expenses."

If you take the predetermined percentage of salary expense approach, then simply include that expense in your financial plan. If the planned revenue is not high enough to cover the planned expenses and still get the desired profit, then this forms the basis of your bonus plan objectives. Increase the revenue line or decrease the expense lines accordingly and create bonus objectives that tie to these changes.

Otherwise, work backward into a bonus pool as follows:

1. Start with the end in mind. How much profit do you expect?
2. How much expense do you expect, exclusive of bonus payments?
3. How much revenue do you expect?

4. If there is more planned revenue than is necessary to cover expenses and meet profit expectations, the difference is a good place to start in defining your bonus pool.

5. If not, you have to first adjust expectations until you have a realistic plan. Now, if the numbers all look right, you have to put your thumb in the air and simply state, "My bonus pool shall be X."

6. Now add that expense in and once again adjust the revenue and expense lines so that your profit expectations remain intact. Again, the changes represent a good starting point for defining bonus plan objectives.

Now that you know your bonus pool, you can divvy it up accordingly among those who will have formal bonus plans, and then document specifically on the bonus plan what the maximum payout will be. Finally, divide the total payout according to how you weighted each objective.

For example, if the total payout is $1,000, objective one is weighted at 50 percent, and objectives two and three are each 25 percent, then the total payout for objective one is $500, while objectives two and three each pay out $250.

Again, you want to take this approach because all-or-nothing plans can be very demoralizing. In this example, objective one is clearly more important than two and three. Suppose objective one is met, but two and three are not met, so you don't pay anything at all. Didn't you get some value from objective one being met? You did if you planned appropriately. Is that worth something to you or the company? It should be. So should you reward your staff for it? Probably.

Next, determine a gatekeeper and an accelerator for the plan. A gatekeeper is a minimum threshold for an objective that must be met in order for there to be any payout.

It is fair to say, "100 percent of the objective has to be met or else there is no payout," but I advise against it. It can be pretty deflating to bust one's hump, get to 99.9 percent of the target, and hear the words, "Better luck next year, chump."

But perhaps more importantly, I very much like a rule of thumb of determining what is within reasonable expectations, then adding a 10 percent stretch factor to it and calling it a bonus objective. It gets people to aim a little higher. In the end, they might only hit half of the stretch, but that is still 5 percent better than you expected, in your heart of hearts.

If you use this approach to setting bonus objectives, then you must use a gatekeeper that is something less than 100 percent or suffer the fate of being called a greedy jerko. Don't be a greedy jerko.

For example, say your gatekeeper is 80 percent. That is to say that 80 percent of the bonus objective must be met in order to receive 80 percent of the bonus payout associated with that objective. Anything less than 80 percent yields no payout. Ninety percent pays 90 percent, and 100 percent achievement yields 100 percent.

In the $1,000 example, suppose objective one was 100 percent achieved, objective two was 90 percent achieved, and objective three was 80 percent achieved. Then the bonus plan would pay $500, $225, and $200 respectively, for a total of $925.

But why should I pay for someone not meeting bonus objectives? Because if you did this right, you got more than $925 worth of added bonus to your bottom line that you would not have otherwise realized. In other words, it didn't cost you a dime to pay someone that $925, and what you got in return for that no-cost bonus was the behavior you wanted in the first place; you have managed the behavior to fit the strategic direction.

Pay-for-Performance Plans

I have to admit that when I first heard of pay-for-performance plans, or P4P, I was skeptical. The notion was literally foreign to me, as I learned about it on a business trip to a business process outsourcing facility in India. Simply put, a P4P plan pays financial incentives for better outcomes.

We could see it was working in India by improving behavior, morale, production, and the bottom line. I say again, even though it resulted in paying beyond the base pay, it was improving the bottom line. And, again, when you think of it in those terms, it doesn't cost a single dime to run a properly defined P4P plan.

So we decided to bring the concept home and implement it in the business I was running, which by that time had exceeded its $50 million initial target and was on its way toward $90 million.

In the course of that growth, the operation had gone from being pretty evenly split between technology professionals, knowledge-processing professionals, and business process laborers (wage earners), to having more than 50 percent business process laborers.

With a new majority in our workforce, we were forced to think differently about our incentives. A salaried program designer who makes a pretty comfortable living gets excited about things like receiving training on the latest must-have-on-the-résumé technologies. Meanwhile, a slightly-better-than-minimum-wage earner gets pretty excited about a few extra bucks or not having to spend money on gas one day out of the week. So we rightly determined that a P4P program for the wage earners made a lot of sense.

We implemented a P4P program that was 100 percent self-funded. Achievements had to, at a bare minimum, match the associated payouts dollar for dollar. If we paid someone an extra $25, we would have to save at least $25. It worked great. In the end, we were able to reduce our head count by 4 percent (through attrition instead of layoffs). We improved the bottom line by more than the cost of the P4P payouts, and we put a little extra money in the pockets of those who needed it the most.

But as one of my former directors said, "A key point to remember is that everyone is motivated by different things. I have many employees who couldn't care less about P4P. It's critical to invest time to determine what makes each employee tick and develop plans to get the most out of everyone."

P4P plans can take on many forms. You should play around with the idea. Talk to non-competing firms that have implemented P4P plans. Do some research. And then ask your employees (audible gasp). Never, ever presume to know what motivates them. You should never implement a one-size-fits-all P4P program, because no P4P program will motivate everyone eligible to receive it.

Conversely, you cannot implement a unique P4P plan for every individual. So do what makes sense for each organization or team that will participate in a P4P, and shoot for providing some level of satisfaction to some majority of the recipients.

Tweak it as you go. We found that when we first implemented the plan, even though it was self-funding from the start, we actually set targets too low. So we continuously but reasonably tweaked the plan.

As my former director so aptly put it, "Everyone is motivated by different things."

P4P is just one tool in your arsenal. That arsenal should consist of many tools. Some will cost nothing. Some may look like an expense on your profit and loss statement. But if you design them well, they don't really cost anything because they save expenses or generate revenue. Still others may truly be expense items that buy you good will. In all cases, the goal is to influence the behaviors that you want or need in order to realize your vision.

So think very carefully about what that behavior is, and what behaviors your rewards programs truly reward.

■ THE CHAPTER 5 WRAP

In his article entitled "How to Inspire Workplace Behaviors to Get Better Results,"[6] Guy Harris reiterates that we can only influence, not control behavior.

He gives some pretty sound advice when he suggests that the first step is to identify the behaviors that will create the desired results. From there it's critical to monitor and measure results, adjusting accordingly as you go.

In this chapter, we identified and discussed the three pillars of behavior management: desire, emotion, and knowledge, and the importance of each one to your behavior management strategy.

We also discussed five common myths about behavior management, including the myth that a behavior management strategy necessarily costs money. In fact, the opposite can be true for positive reinforcement techniques, like formal peer recognition programs. Additionally, when defined and implemented appropriately, other tools, like bonus and P4P plans, can and should positively contribute to the top and bottom line, resulting in a net cost of zero and a net gain of something greater than zero.

Be careful to design bonus and P4P plans that encourage the right behaviors. Poorly designed plans can have the exact opposite effect to what was intended. And finally, no one thing will motivate and inspire the

---

6 Guy Harris, "How to Inspire Workplace Behaviors to Get
   Better Results," businessrelationshiprx.com (blog), May 7, 2010,
   http://businessrelationshiprx.com/performance-management/
   how-to-inspire-workplace-behaviors-to-get-better-results.

desired behavior in everyone. Your strategy should include multiple tools and techniques.

Regardless of how you approach behavior management, it starts at the top. It starts with you.

In the next chapter, we discuss the business plan, which is different from the strategic plan.

Before proceeding, please answer the following questions:

1. How do you manage behavior?
2. Does your reward and recognition program include monetary, nonmonetary, formal, and informal components?
3. Does your reward and recognition program encourage the desired behavior? Are you sure?

SIX

THE BUSINESS PLAN

You were born to win, but to be a winner,
you must plan to win, prepare to win, and expect to win.
ZIG ZIGLER, AMERICAN AUTHOR
AND MOTIVATIONAL SPEAKER

A business plan and a strategic plan are two related but separate things. A business plan is typically created for a single operating year, while a strategic plan looks well beyond. The strategic plan focuses on where the business is headed in the future. The business plan focuses on how it operates day to day.

Using a football analogy, you might think of strategy as how your team will get to and win the Super Bowl. You determine the type of offense and defense your team will need. You consider your opponents for the season, your home games, and your away games. You determine the skill positions and coaches you will need to get there. The business plan is more like the Sunday game plan. It is more tactical and lays out the details for how you're just going to win this one game, which in turn supports your strategy to win the Super Bowl.

Can you imagine a team winning the Super Bowl without having a strategy to get there? Based on sheer talent and luck, a team might win the occasional game, but luck and talent are not enough to take it all the way to wearing that new hat and T-shirt after the Super Bowl concludes. No ticker tape parade. No pretty ring. Someone else has strategized and planned better than your team. They are the new lords of the rings.

■ WHY WOULD YOU NOT HAVE A BUSINESS PLAN?

Some estimates say that as many as eight out of ten new businesses fail within the first eighteen months. More conservative estimates say that about half of new business start-ups are still in business four to five years later. In either case, the likelihood of business failure is very high, so anything that improves the odds should be welcomed by both the business and the investment communities.

Studies prove that good business planning practices more than double the chance of business success. Yet the vast majority of small to medium-sized businesses operate without a formal plan, and only a subset of those follow through by measuring their targeted objectives and adjusting their plans accordingly. Why?

As a consultant, I see some of the common reasons: they just don't know any better, it's just too complicated, and it's just too time-consuming. Translation: it's just too easy *not* to do it.

As with going into the Sunday football game without a game plan, you might get lucky. You might win the game. But you might do so at the risk of serious injury to your players, who aren't well prepared for the opponent. The trauma of the win may be so great that the resulting stress eliminates the thrill of the victory and taints emotions going into the next game.

What's more likely is that the other team wins. They will be better prepared to anticipate your every move, whereas you will constantly be in reaction mode. They will have an answer for everything you can throw at them. Is the risk of losing really worth not planning? The big difference here is, we aren't talking about bragging rights. We are talking about your dream, your livelihood, and that of your family and employees. Are they worth the risk?

Start-up companies that need seed money must create detailed business plans to obtain loans, attract investors, and launch successful crowdfunding campaigns. But the process is often tedious and forgotten after the initial requirement has been established. Good planning practices are performed continuously, not in a once and done fashion.

■ THE BUSINESS IS ART BUSINESS
PLAN TEMPLATE

Business owners and leaders need tools that help them easily articulate, revise, and track plans and objectives on an ongoing basis. There are any number of templates, processes, and methodologies available, many for free and found easily from an Internet search. But, again, in my experience these plans are often complex and text based, and they can be as worthless and frustrating to use as the large strategic plan templates.

So I developed a simple, table-driven business plan template as part of the Business Is ART framework. It includes a one-page summary that I strongly urge every small to medium-sized business to use. If you use nothing else, use this one-page summary. In so doing, you will already be well ahead of the majority of your competition. Ideally, however, you will complete the details within the business plan first, and then create the summary from it. These next few pages show the business plan template.

You do not have to feel limited to the components I have included in this template. Add whatever you want, to your little heart's content. This template merely represents the minimum of what you need to consider in your plan.

The plan template includes the following:

- Executive summary
- Product sales and marketing plan
- Operating plan
- Staffing plan
- Financial plan
- Conclusion

THE BUSINESS IS ART BUSINESS PLAN

Executive Summary

COMPANY/BUSINESS UNIT

> Brief description of company, organization, or business unit

MISSION

> Brief description of what the business does

PURPOSE

> Brief description of why it does it (focus on passion, emotion, appeal)

ONE-YEAR OBJECTIVES/PERFORMANCE METRICS

Complete this table after completing the rest of the plan. Alternatively, for a very simplified plan, complete this table and ignore the rest of the document. Fill in the category from the categories identified in this plan template: 1) product sales and marketing, 2) operating, 3) staffing, 4) financial, or 5) other.

TABLE 6.1. ONE-YEAR OBJECTIVES AND PERFORMANCE METRICS WORKSHEET.

OBJECTIVE/ METRIC	TARGET	KEYS TO SUCCESS	CATEGORY

Product Sales and Marketing Plan
Determine the marketing budget. Possible methods:

1. Set your budget as a percentage of revenue that you can afford, then complete this plan.
2. Complete this plan first, estimate the cost, then decide whether you are willing to spend that amount. If so, that becomes your budget. If not, adjust the plan accordingly.

PRODUCTS AND SERVICES: WHY, HOW, WHAT?
For each major product or service, complete a row in the following table:

TABLE 6.2. PRODUCTS AND SERVICES WORKSHEET.

WHY	HOW	WHAT	DESCRIPTION/NOTES
Why does the customer want or need it?	How does the product or service fill the want or need?	What is the product or service?	Describe the product or service, or add notes if necessary.

MARKET ANALYSIS

For each major product or service, complete a row in the following table:

TABLE 6.3. MARKET ANALYSIS WORKSHEET.

PRODUCT/ SERVICE	MARKET SIZE	MARKET TRENDS	MARKET SHARE	COMPETITORS
	Quantify the market.	What is the latest trend?	What is your market share %?	Who competes with this product or service?

SALES AND MARKETING PLAN OBJECTIVES

The primary goals of a marketing plan are to generate awareness, sales, and revenue and to improve customer relations, public relations, and public perception. Use the following table to list specific, measurable objectives of the marketing plan.

TABLE 6.4. SALES AND MARKETING OBJECTIVES WORKSHEET.

NAME/ DESCRIPTION	METRIC	TARGET	TARGET DATE
Name and description of objective. e.g., Increase new customer sales.	How will the objective be measured? e.g., New customers.	Quantify the objective target. e.g., 5	Date when the objective will be achieved. e.g., 2015/12/31

SALES AND MARKETING STRATEGY

For each major product or service, complete a row in the following table:

TABLE 6.5. SALES AND MARKETING STRATEGY WORKSHEET.

PRODUCT/ SERVICE	PRICE	QUALITY	CHANNEL	PROMOTION
	What is the pricing strategy? High price, competitive, low price, etc.?	Will the marketing strategy focus on quality, quantity, etc.? If so, how?	What are the sales channels?	How will the product or service be promoted?

SALES FORECAST

For each major product or service (or client), complete a row in the following table:

TABLE 6.6. SALES FORECAST WORKSHEET.

PRODUCT/ SERVICE	PIPELINE	PROB- ABILITY	WEIGHTED PIPELINE	REVENUE THIS YEAR
	Quantify both identified and unidentified potential sales in dollars.	Estimate likelihood of the sale (25%, 50%, 75%, 90%).	Multiply pipeline by probability.	Estimate the revenue that will be recognized this fiscal year from the total in the weighted pipeline cell.

■ OPERATING PLAN

Organization Structure

Even small organizations will benefit from an organization structure that clearly identifies who is responsible for what. Use the organizational chart below as a template.

FIGURE 6.1. ORGANIZATIONAL CHART TEMPLATE.

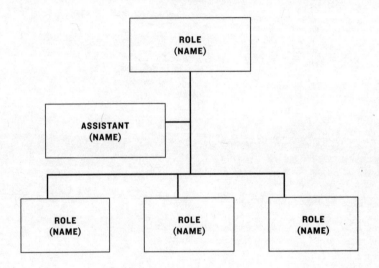

PRODUCTION METHODOLOGY

Briefly describe your methodology for each of the following. Copy and paste separate tables if necessary for unique products or services, then identify any investments required to establish or improve production. Include any investments appropriately in the financial plan.

TABLE 6.7. PRODUCTION METHODOLOGY WORKSHEET.

QUALITY CONTROL

CUSTOMER SERVICE

INVENTORY CONTROL

PRODUCT DEVELOPMENT

INVESTMENTS

CURRENT FACILITIES AND INFRASTRUCTURE

List your current locations and briefly describe any special considerations for facilities or infrastructure. Note any investments planned or required under "special infrastructure considerations" and include costs as appropriate in the financial plan.

TABLE 6.8. CURRENT FACILITIES AND INFRASTRUCTURE WORKSHEET.

LOCATION	PRIMARY PURPOSE	SPECIAL INFRASTRUCTURE CONSIDERATIONS

PLANNED FACILITIES AND INFRASTRUCTURE

List planned locations (if applicable) and briefly describe any special considerations.

TABLE 6.9. PLANNED FACILITIES AND INFRASTRUCTURE WORKSHEET.

LOCATION	PRIMARY PURPOSE	SPECIAL INFRASTRUCTURE CONSIDERATIONS

OPERATING OBJECTIVES

The primary goal of an operating plan is to meet the demand for your product or service within defined quality standards.

TABLE 6.10. OPERATING OBJECTIVES WORKSHEET.

NAME/ DESCRIPTION	METRIC	TARGET	TARGET DATE
Name and description of objective.	How will the objective be measured?	Quantify the objective target.	Date by which the objective should be achieved.

Staffing Plan
STAFFING AND RECRUITING

TABLE 6.11. STAFFING AND RECRUITING WORKSHEET.

RESOURCES REQUIRED TO SUPPORT PLANNED REVENUE	CURRENT STAFFING LEVELS	REQUIRED STAFFING CHANGES	ESTIMATED RECRUITING OR SEVERANCE COSTS
Give the estimated resources by product or service.		Insert a positive or negative number.	

TRAINING PLAN

TABLE 6.12. TRAINING PLAN WORKSHEET.

TRAINING	TRAINING COST PER INDIVIDUAL	NUMBER OF RESOURCES TO ATTEND TRAINING	TOTAL COST OF TRAINING

BONUS AND INCENTIVE PLAN

- For formal bonus or incentive plans, I recommend using three meaningful objectives to determine payouts.
  - > One objective should tie to overall company performance.
  - > A second should tie to a function or organization within the company.
  - > The third should tie specifically to the individual's role.
- The purpose of the following table is to plan the bonus and incentive program and tie it to objectives from the business plan. A separate template should be used for detailed bonus planning purposes.
  - > The plan should identify who participates,
  - > Determine a gatekeeper (e.g., 80 percent of the objective must be met),
  - > Make payouts in accordance with results (e.g., if 85 percent of the objective is met, pay 85 percent of the bonus associated with that objective), and
  - > Identify accelerators (if more than 100 percent of the objective is met, determine what percentage over 100 percent will be paid out).
- Set an overall budget (e.g., 10 percent of total wage or salary expense) and include that as appropriate in the financial plan.

TABLE 6.13. BONUS AND INCENTIVE PLAN WORKSHEET.

BONUS/ INCENTIVE NAME	OBJECTIVE 1	OBJECTIVE 2	OBJECTIVE 3

OTHER RETENTION PLANS

List other things you will do to shape behavior and create the desired company culture. This is also a good place to identify any corporate social responsibility plans (programs in which the company will participate). These activities and awards lead to employee retention (and attraction) and can often be done at little to no cost, for example a quarterly pot luck lunch, lunch-and-learns, or paid time off (over and above standard policy). Be sure to include any estimated costs in the financial plan.

TABLE 6.14. OTHER RETENTION PLANS WORKSHEET.

PROGRAM, EVENT, OR AWARD	QUALIFICATION
	Identify anything that serves as a qualifier to whether the event, program, or award will actually occur.

Financial Plan

ASSUMPTIONS, RISKS, AND MITIGATION

TABLE 6.15. ASSUMPTIONS, RISKS, AND MITIGATION WORKSHEET.

ASSUMPTION	RISK	LIKELIHOOD (OF RISK)	MITIGATION STRATEGY
List any major assumptions that need to be true in order to meet financial plan targets.	List any risks that may threaten those assumptions.	Rate the likelihood as high, medium, or low.	Discuss how to mitigate against the risk.

ASSUMPTION	RISK	LIKELIHOOD (OF RISK)	MITIGATION STRATEGY

ACCOUNTING OBJECTIVES OR PERFORMANCE METRICS

TABLE 6.16. ACCOUNTING OBJECTIVES WORKSHEET.

OBJECTIVES/METRICS	TARGET	DUE BY
List any objectives typically associated with accounting practices such as accounts receivable, payables, and cash flow.	What do you plan to achieve?	Typically at year end, but if you have quarterly, biannual, or other objectives, identify them here.

PROFIT AND LOSS

Insert from your financial system, or use this worksheet to make modifications:

FIGURE 6.2. PROFIT AND LOSS WORKSHEET.

		2 YEARS PREVIOUS	1 YEAR PREVIOUS	PLAN YEAR
REVENUE	Product 1			
	Product 2			
	Product n			
Total Revenue		Total	Total	Total
COST OF LABOR	Labor			
	Benefits			
	Bonus/Incentive Pay			
Total Cost of Labor		Total	Total	Total
% of Revenue (Total Revenue ÷ Total Cost of Labor)				
OTHER DIRECT COSTS	Contract Services			
	Training			
	Travel & Entertainment			
	Materials			
	Other			
Total Other Direct Costs		Total	Total	Total
% of Revenue (Total Other Direct Costs ÷ Total Revenue)				
Total Direct Costs (Total Cost of Labor + Total Other Direct Costs)				
Gross Profit (Total Revenue ÷ Total Direct Costs)				
Gross Margin (Gross Profit ÷ Total Revenue)				

		2 YEARS PREVIOUS	1 YEAR PREVIOUS	PLAN YEAR
SELLING & MARKETING EXPENSES	Labor			
	Benefits			
	Bonus/Incentive Pay			
	Training			
	Professional Services			
	Travel & Entertainment			
	Campaigns			
	Other			
Total Selling & Marketing Expenses		Total	Total	Total
% of Revenue (Total Selling & Marketing Expenses ÷ Total Revenue)				
GENERAL & ADMINISTRA-TIVE EXPENSES	Labor			
	Benefits			
	Bonus/Incentive Pay			
	Training			
	Professional Services			
	Travel & Entertainment			
	Rent/Lease/Facilities			
	Other			
Total G&A Expenses		Total	Total	Total
% of Revenue (Total G&A Expenses ÷ Total Revenue)				
Total SG&A (Total G&A Expenses + Total Selling & Marketing Expenses)				
Total Costs & Expenses (Total SG&A + Total Direct Costs)				
Net Profit (Total Revenue − Total Costs & Expenses)				
Profit Margin (Net Profit ÷ Total Revenue)				

Conclusion

> Make any notes or statements in conclusion of the business plan.

■ I HAVE A PLAN—NOW WHAT?

> *Being busy does not always mean real work. The*
> *object of all work is production or accomplishment*
> *and to either of these ends there must be forethought,*
> *system, planning, intelligence, and honest purpose,*
> *as well as perspiration. Seeming to do is not doing.*
> THOMAS EDISON, AMERICAN INVENTOR

Now it's time to get to work. What kind of work depends on what the business plan was created for. If it's for a start-up looking for investors, start sharing it with potential investors. If it's to better run an existing company, start executing the plan. The best way to do that is to keep it in front of you and your team. Do this by regularly reviewing plan progress.

I am a one-person consulting business. I don't have a paid team and I don't have a board. But I still act like I do. I have designated a trusted advisor as my "chairman of the board." Every Friday we meet, usually over lunch or a late afternoon cocktail, to review the plan.

What went well this week? What did not? Where did I make progress? How does the plan need to be adjusted? This helps to keep me honest with myself and focused on what it is I want to accomplish.

The point is this: you are not too small to have a plan, and you are not too small to have a team with whom to review plan progress and adjust accordingly. Many people feel they just don't have time for it, but that is nonsense. In my case, the meeting takes about an hour, we have it over lunch or a glass of wine, and I can't even begin to quantify the productivity gains that result from the review.

Business Is ART is largely about articulating what it is you want to accomplish, and when you write it down, you do accomplish things much faster. In the summer of 2014, my strategic plan included a strategic objective of publishing a book by October 1, 2015; a book that at that time was only a concept with nothing more than a title.

We met weekly to review my plan, so each week, I wanted to have something to report and show that I had made some progress. Inevitably, I would make a comment like "Next week I am thinking about doing X," and that would spawn discussion about better ways to approach it, or perhaps even new directions if the initial thought no longer made as much sense after our discussion.

Four months later, the draft manuscript was 90 percent complete, I had a team of people coaching, researching, and reviewing materials, and I was negotiating with a publisher. Business Is ART was subsequently scheduled for a late September or early October 2015 release.

That would not have happened had I not *articulated* the plan, *revised* the plan as I moved forward, and *tracked* my progress. But it moved much more quickly because I reviewed each step with someone. I saved countless, countless hours and months because of this review.

Plus, food and wine is fun.

■ WELL, *THAT* DIDN'T WORK!

The more time you spend contemplating what you should have done . . . you lose valuable time planning what you can and will do.
LIL WAYNE, RECORDING ARTIST AND ENTERTAINER

When you try to change large institutions, as I did with the company we wanted to drive to $50 million, there will be failures. You will have missed something. The ball won't bounce your way. Something will happen, and in fact, things usually happen in multiples. The best thing you can do for yourself, your team, and your organization is to stay calm and be prepared to make some very tough choices.

One of the subgroups that had been part of the company I was hired to run had developed a culture of finger pointing. It was odd, because within that team they were very quick to point fingers. But if anyone outside that team pointed at anyone in the team, there would be hell to pay.

I think this team created the phrase "Oh no—you *didn't!*" (finger wag, finger wag).

It drove me nuts, and the only way to break it was to 1) not accept it and 2) not behave that way myself. Trust me, there were plenty of times I wanted to point a finger and ask (loudly) "What were you thinking?!"

But instead we set the tone and expectation that stuff will happen. Things won't go according to plan. Mistakes will be made. We will fail from time to time. All that mattered was learning how and why it went wrong so that we could fix it and devise a plan for avoiding it in the future.

When my son was about twelve, I came walking through the living room carrying a basket of freshly folded laundry. I am one of those ninnies who will load up as many grocery bags as possible on my arms to avoid a second trip out to the car. This leaves me waddling and struggling to get up that next step, but by golly, I get them all in one trip! The same is true of laundry. Small basket? Lots of clothes? No problem. Your chin was made to hold the clothes in place while your arms extend as far down as they can, holding the basket.

On this particular day, there was one problem with my methodology. An ottoman. I tripped over it. Clothes went flying everywhere, and I landed on my face in front of my son, who sat for a moment in sheer terror of the outburst that would surely follow. But instead, I started laughing at myself, which caused him to belly laugh to the point of tears.

Once he caught his breath he said, "I was so sure you were going to be furious."

Lesson learned. It is not how you fall, it is truly how you pick yourself up after the fall. In this simple example, we turned what could have been an unpleasant memory into a great one. And we had a great moment together in the process.

The same can be true in business. True, the ramifications of falling down in business can be much more serious than a bruised ego resulting from tripping over a piece of furniture, but turning it into a positive learning experience can be just as emotionally rewarding.

The bottom line is: don't dwell on it. Simply learn from it and move on rapidly, because there is another load in the dryer, just waiting to be folded.

The plan *will* fail. That it does is not the issue. How you respond is.

■ PREPARE YOURSELF FOR TOUGH CHOICES

Without a plan, it becomes easy to brush aside or ignore the tough choices you will have to make. It isn't all fun and games. The most heart-wrenching of these will be when you determine you are overstaffed, or perhaps not right-staffed. You may have someone on the team who really should not be there... but doggone it, you just *love* this person. I am not advocating cold-hearted mafia-style, "It's just business" business, but sometimes... it is.

The danger of keeping people on board out of love, sympathy, or just not wanting to whack someone is that you are not just doing a disservice to yourself and your business, you are doing a disservice to others who do have the skills, attitude, and productivity—people who closely meet your needs, support your vision, and are capable of executing your business plan. It isn't fair to them.

It also isn't fair to the person you are hanging onto when you shouldn't be. I was in that position once: for months my instincts were telling me the hammer was going to fall, but I was being assured everything was just fine. It wasn't, as I ultimately found out. If my boss had been honest with me about that, I could have worked to change the situation in some way, including seeking employment elsewhere. Once we finally decided to part ways, it was one of the most liberating feelings I had ever had. Sometimes your plan simply can't be executed with the people you have, and that puts undue stress on everyone involved.

There are four examples I'd like to share with you of tough calls that had to be made in our quest to reach $50 million. Having a plan helped bubble those decisions to the top, to where there was no denying them. But, in not all cases did I pull the trigger fast enough, so to speak.

Example 1—Carl Has to Go

Carl (name changed to protect the innocent and keep the civil attorneys at bay) was an institution. He was a sweet, elderly gentleman, well past retirement age. Everyone loved him. I loved him. He was a genuinely nice guy with a twinkle in his eye. But Carl just couldn't keep up with our growth.

His job was to stuff billing statements into envelopes. We modernized our equipment and, while I am sure I am overly simplifying things, Carl had one very key task: make sure the right envelopes are loaded in the stuffer.

We knew Carl wasn't performing very well. But we loved Carl! And he wasn't qualified for anything else that we had to offer. So we kept him on, doing the same job he'd done for years.

Then one day, the wrong statements were stuffed in the wrong envelopes and mailed out. This was very costly and embarrassing. Two clients got severely mad at us, and we had a lot of explaining to do. Just when we were recovering from that, it happened again.

This time, we had no choice but to do what we knew we should have done before the first mistake. We let Carl go. And yes, Carl did sue. But the expense of settling out of court was nothing compared to the business we could have lost, or the consequences if we had sent secure information to the wrong person.

Because we had a plan, it was very clear that Carl could no longer be a part of us because his very presence was harmful to the plan.

Example 2—Debbie Has to Go Now...Not Later
One of the chief finger pointers, and a leader in the aforementioned "Oh no, you didn't" gang, looked at our plans and said, "This is not for me."

I'll call her Debbie. Debbie came to me one day and said that this direction wasn't for her and she would like to resign. This was kind of a relief to me because I was thinking I'd have to let her go. My view of her leadership style was that she would be more effective as a mushroom farmer: feed them crap and keep them in the dark. That is how she treated her employees and clients, and it didn't sit well with me.

When Debbie offered to resign, my reaction should have been to say, "Thank you, and please don't forget to grab your coat on the way out."

But Debbie made me an offer in exchange for her resignation. She offered to stay on for two months while I figured out how to organize and work with clients on the change in leadership. I took the easy way out and said, "Fair enough." It sounded good on paper. She'd quit, saving me the hassle and expense of firing her. There would be no severance package and no potential for a lawsuit. Seemed like a win-win, right? Wrong! Very wrong!

The damage Debbie did in her final two months was deep and lingering. I'm no genius, but I suspect this was her evil plan all along. She then waited a year and went to work for our primary competitor the day after her non-compete clause expired, where she proceeded, unsuccessfully, to try to win customers away from us.

The plan told me that Debbie did not fit because her style did not meet the expectations of leaders for which our plan called. Our plan didn't suit her, and she herself admitted as much. I should have made the tough choice as soon as that was evident. And then when she offered to quit, I should have never struck a deal with her. I should have accepted her resignation effective immediately. I will never, ever make that kind of deal again.

Example 3—Everyone Is Replaceable

Everyone is replaceable, including you and me. All of us. People make a huge mistake when they say out loud, "You can't make it without me." Talk about motivation to do just that.

In this example, I had the plan. I had determined that an "office" that the "Oh no, you didn't" team had opened several years earlier in a remote location was not necessary. I knew what it was telling me to do. And I did it without letting a threatening employee bully me off the decision.

First, this "office" was a rented house. Second, they were using it to run a production server. A production server containing client data *in a rented house.* Probably in the dining room, I'm not really sure. Third, there were two and a half staff positions at this "office," and one staff member was being let go for poor performance. Probably because he was spending too much time in the living room. I don't know.

One of the first organizational moves I made was to centralize technical services instead of having tech support within each of the four businesses we operated. The two and a half guys in this house were moved into this organization and they were annoyed. But whether they were mad or happy was beyond the point.

The point was this: having a production server in a regular old rented house is just plain stupid.

When I announced plans to move that server into our secure data center, and get out of the lease on the house, one guy immediately quit. The one that remained asked to meet with me, to which I agreed. Many people told me that he was a really valuable resource with a strong client relationship, and that we should do all we could to make him happy.

When we met, he told me what an idiot I was (in those words) and that if I didn't change my mind or rent a new office space just for him, he'd quit and take one of our biggest customers with him. I gave him Debbie's number and suggested he call her for a ride home because he no longer worked for us.

The result was that the new technical team found its productivity actually increased in the absence of the two and a half dwellers of the former rented house. In addition to the house being a really bad idea, they were creating work, not production results. Clearly, our plan did not call for the creation of non-value-adding work.

Example 4—Sometimes You Have to Fire the Client
Our quest for $50 million would not be easy, and we couldn't afford to lose any clients along the way. Or could we? In developing our business plan, we determined that one client in particular, we will call it an anonymous government agency in the state of Wisconsin (even though I love visiting that state), was a truly bad client.

They constantly demanded that we deliver well beyond the scope of our contract. They were never happy. They constantly spoke ill of our services to other would-be clients. And the account was not profitable. We felt in this case that actually making this client an advocate was an impossible chore, and that no matter what we did, they would be a detractor.

So when our contract came up for renewal, we chose not to submit a proposal, effectively firing the client. The team, and my salesperson especially, was shocked that I'd do such a thing, but once it was over, there was a huge sigh of relief. That burdensome client was gone and we could focus on more important things. We could focus on our plan.

A year later, the salesperson said to me, "When you let them go, I thought you were crazy. But now I see the method to your madness."

Sometimes, you have to fire the client.

■ THE CHAPTER 6 WRAP

In this chapter, we discussed the difference between a strategic plan and a business plan. The strategic plan focuses on where the business or organization is headed over the long haul, while the business plan usually looks out over a single operating year and focuses on how the business will run day to day in support of the strategy.

The Business Is ART framework includes a simplified, table-driven template that asks you to think about the minimal components of a business plan. It also provides a one-page executive summary that you should complete after filling in the details of the business plan, but if you do nothing else, at least use the one-page summary as a watered-down business plan. It is far better than nothing.

Finally, we discussed how a business plan can help you make decisions, sometimes tough ones, that might be more difficult to identify or make in the absence of a plan. The plan helps them bubble to the surface.

There is no way to objectively know if your business plan is working unless you track performance metrics. The next chapter discusses this in more detail.

Before proceeding, please answer the following questions:

1. Do you have a formal business plan?
2. If not, why not?
3. Can you think of a time when having a business plan would have helped you? If so, can you quantify how much it cost you (either in lost opportunity or in cost to deliver) to not have one?

SEVEN

THE IMPORTANCE
OF METRICS

*The only man I know who behaves sensibly is
my tailor; he takes my measurements anew each
time he sees me. The rest go on with their old
measurements and expect me to fit them.*

GEORGE BERNARD SHAW, IRISH PLAYWRIGHT AND A
CO-FOUNDER OF THE LONDON SCHOOL OF ECONOMICS

Without proper metrics, you can't determine how to
move forward. You can't be certain the suit will fit until
you try it on and find that it doesn't. It seems appropriate to include a George Bernard Shaw quote in a book
entitled *Business Is ART*. He is, after all, one of the greatest
playwrights ever to put pen to paper. It seems even more
appropriate to include his quote in a business book, given
he was a cofounder of the London School of Economics.

In college, I played the role of Snobby Price in Shaw's
Major Barbara. Snobby is a dirty little character who

confesses to sins he didn't commit in order to be "for-given" (and get favors). In one exchange with Rummy Mitchens, a female character, Snobby says he's going to confess how he used to beat his poor old mother.

Rummy basically says, "You used to beat your mother?" and Snobby says no, but that's what he's going to tell them because that's what they want to hear. Rummy's response is that it is unfair that men can sit around the table, tell their lies, and "be made much of for it."

I love this exchange in the context of Business Is ART for two reasons. One, being an ARTist and painting your picture is a great deal of what Business Is ART is about. Snobby doesn't currently have a plan that will work, so he revises his plan by revising his persona. Two, Business Is ART is also about tracking your prog-ress toward achieving your plans. Rummy's response about people sitting around the table and telling lies is exactly why it is important to track things: to reduce the likelihood of lying to ourselves or to others, whether purposely or inadvertently.

There is an expression that numbers don't lie. My experience is that they can certainly be made to lie. But if you are less than rigorous in measuring progress or have ill-defined metrics, the opportunities to lie increase significantly.

Without evidence that you have carefully collected, it is easy to lie to employees, customers, investors, and other stakeholders. In fact, it may be immoral or even illegal. But unless you're just a born liar, the more likely scenario is that, without properly defined metrics, you will lie to yourself.

Simon Cowell, producer and talent scout extraordinaire, perhaps best known for his work on shows such as *Pop Idol, American Idol, Britain's Got Talent,* and *The X Factor*, says, "Create the hype, but don't ever believe it."

Cowell was twice named one of the top one hundred most influential people in the world by *Time* magazine, so he probably knows a thing or two about hype. One can argue against his sometimes ruthless bluntness, made famous with his lead-in (and book by the same title) "I don't mean to be rude, but..."

But, from an integrity point of view, he just shoots completely honestly with contestants on these shows and asks them to take an honest look at themselves when many of them, very clearly, do not have what it takes to be a pop star or were decidedly not talented vocally.

This is one of the main points to performance metrics. We can't continue to make progress if we can't honestly determine how we are doing now. We can't honestly shoot for pop stardom if we can't honestly determine what qualifications we have now and what qualifications we need to obtain.

In his book *Measuring Performance*, Bob Frost puts it this way with respect to performance metrics: "There is no more essential and valuable step in performance management than translating the overall direction of your organization into concrete and meaningful terms that people understand."[1]

---

1 Bob Frost, *Measuring Performance* (Dallas, Texas: Measurement International, 2000).

In other words, the most important thing you can do is turn (translate) all of those visions, goals, and plans (direction of your organization) into performance metrics (concrete and meaningful terms).

■ TRACKING PERFORMANCE IS A DISCIPLINE

Lou Holtz, a legendary football coach and sports commentator said, "Without self-discipline, success is impossible, period."

Let's take his assertion and apply it to metrics. Measuring and tracking performance is absolutely a discipline. It is only fun when we get to see charts and numbers that show us that we successfully got from here to there. But they don't always show that, and they never will if we don't identify how we will measure performance and track progress.

COACH LOU HOLTZ—MOTIVATIONAL SPEAKER

I once had the opportunity to hear Lou Holtz speak at a business conference. He was inspiring, entertaining, educational, and funny—everything you'd want in a keynote speaker.

Coach Holtz had a significant speech impediment, something that would have stopped many people who would otherwise make a living out of talking, teaching, coaching, and communicating dead in their tracks. He didn't let it deter him and turned it into something of a trademark. When he speaks, you know it's him without looking or seeing his name in print.

In his presentations he talks about it and dismisses it jokingly. Even though he only did so in somewhat passing fashion at this particular event, it sent a powerful message. It said to me, "Your perceived limitations don't matter. Take what you were given and mold it into something better—something that works for you—without changing who you are."

One of my favorite parts of his presentation was a joke he told about a time he and his wife were out for dinner. The waiter, obviously not a fan, said to him, "Hey, Coach. Do you know the difference between cereal and Lou Holtz?"

Amused, Holtz said, "No. What's the difference?"

The waiter replied, "The cereal deserves to be in a bowl."

He said this really made him mad, and the longer dinner went on, the angrier he got. He told his wife he was going to say something to this rude waiter, but she urged him to keep his cool. He acquiesced to her request for calm.

But when dinner was over and the waiter brought the check, Coach Holtz said to him, "Hey, do you know the difference between a bookie and Lou Holtz?"

"No," replied the waiter.

Coach said, "The bookie will give you a tip."

■ KEY PERFORMANCE INDICATORS

The discipline to track performance metrics, commonly referred to as key performance indicators, or KPIs, has to come from within, or by directive (from a board, for example). But what do you do once you decide to track performance? If you are not sure, start with what you have done thus far in the Business Is ART process. By now, you should have a very good idea of what defines success and what is important to you.

The book *Key Performance Indicators*, by Bernard Marr, identifies and defines seventy-five KPIs in great detail. It is an excellent source for helping you identify your own KPIs. It even tells you how to measure, collect, or calculate each one.

But seventy-five is a lot of KPIs. This message will be repeated later, but it is important, so listen carefully... you don't need seventy-five KPIs. Most businesses don't need many at all, but it is critical to have a few, maybe four to twelve. It's just as critical for you to determine what KPIs are important to you and to your business. Some of the easy ones include revenue and profit. Cost per unit sold might be another. These are basic KPIs that every business should be measuring.

Don't be overwhelmed; the purpose of reviewing a wide array of KPIs is to expand your knowledge and think about how else you might measure success. I'm not suggesting that you measure dozens of KPIs.

Marr smartly divides KPIs into six categories that he calls "perspectives," as follows:

- Financial
- Customer
- Sales and marketing
- Operational
- Employee
- Corporate and social responsibility

His approach fits very nicely with the ProCESS Strategy discussed in chapter 3. As a refresher, the ProCESS-based strategic plan includes four principal areas of focus: profitability, customer satisfaction, employee satisfaction, and social responsibility. These four areas of focus directly align with Marr's categorical perspectives of financial, customer, employee, and corporate and social responsibility, respectively.

Within the Business Is ART framework, sales and marketing and operational goals and objectives are key components of the business plan discussed in chapter 6.

Some of the KPIs identified in Marr's book are complex and require a level of sophistication in data-gathering capability that goes beyond that of the typical small or medium-sized business. For the purpose of this book (and accompanying software), I've slimmed Marr's list down a bit and added a few KPIs of my own.

Marr's book defines most of these and more in detail, but the following table provides my modified list and a quick definition for reference:

TABLE 7.1. KEY PERFORMANCE INDICATORS.

CATEGORY	KPI	SHORT DEFINITION
Financial	Net profit	Bottom line financial results ($).
Financial	Net profit margin	Profit generated for each dollar in revenue (%).
Financial	Gross profit	Revenue minus cost of goods sold ($).
Financial	Gross profit margin	Gross profit divided by revenue (%).
Financial	Operating profit	Profit after cost of goods and overhead ($).

CATEGORY	KPI	SHORT DEFINITION
Financial	Operating profit margin	Operating profit divided by revenue (%).
Financial	EBITDA	Earnings before interest, taxes, depreciation, and amortization ($).
Financial	Revenue growth rate	Revenue reported this period as compared to a previous period (%).
Financial	Return on investment	(Gain from investment minus cost of investment) divided by cost of investment (%).
Financial	Debt to equity ratio	Total liabilities divided by total equity.
Financial	Cash on hand	Average balance of cash in a given period.
Financial	Average accounts receivable	Average days it takes to collect a receivable.
Financial	Accounts receivable turnover ratio	Net sales divided by average receivables.
Customer	Net promoter score	Percentage of customers who are "promoters" minus the percentage of customers who are detractors.
Customer	Customer retention rate	Number of customers at the beginning of the period divided by those who are still customers at the end of the period.
Customer	Customer satisfaction index	Customer satisfaction as measured by survey results (usually numeric, e.g., scale of one to ten).
Customer	Customer turnover rate	Lost customers over a period divided by customers remaining at end of period.
Customer	Customer complaints	Frequency and resolution time of customer complaints.
Sales and marketing	Market growth rate	Total sales in the market this year divided by total sales in the market last year.
Sales and marketing	Market share	Percentage of the defined market that you hold.
Sales and marketing	New accounts/ customers	Number of new customers in a defined period.

CATEGORY	KPI	SHORT DEFINITION
Sales and marketing	Cost per lead	Total spent on marketing campaign divided by the number of leads generated.
Sales and marketing	Search engine rankings	A website's position in the search engine rankings.
Sales and marketing	Click through rate	A ratio showing how often people who see your ad end up clicking it.
Sales and marketing	Page views	The total number of views on an Internet page.
Sales and marketing	Bounce rates	Total number of visits on one page only divided by total number of visits.
Operational	Six Sigma level	See Six Sigma process level.
Operational	Capacity use rate	Actual capacity in a given time period divided by possible capacity in the same time period.
Operational	Order fulfillment cycle time	Time from customer authorization of sale to customer receipt of product.
Operational	Delivery in full, on time rate	Units or orders delivered in full, on time divided by total units or orders shipped.
Operational	Inventory shrinkage rate	(Inventory you should have per records minus actual inventory) divided by inventory you should have.
Operational	Project schedule variance	Scheduled completion time minus actual completion time.
Operational	Project cost variance	Scheduled project cost minus actual project cost.
Operational	Rework level	Number of items reworked divided by number of items inspected.
Operational	Quality	Good pieces divided by total pieces.
Operational	Equipment availability	Operating time divided by planned production time.
Operational	Equipment performance	Ideal cycle time divided by (operating time divided by total pieces).
Operational	Overall equipment effectiveness	Availability times performance times quality.

CATEGORY	KPI	SHORT DEFINITION
Operational	First contact resolution	Number of queries divided by number of calls times 100.
Employee	Human capital value added	Revenue minus ((total costs minus employee costs) divided by number of full-time equivalent employees).
Employee	Revenue per employee	Revenue divided by number of full-time equivalent employees.
Employee	Employee satisfaction index	Employee satisfaction as measured by survey results (usually numeric, e.g., scale of one to five).
Employee	Staff advocacy score	Percentage of employees who are advocates minus the percentage of employees who are detractors.
Employee	Employee churn rate	Total number of employees to leave in a period divided by average number of employees employed in the same period.
Employee	Average employee tenure	Sum of all tenure divided by total number of employees.
Employee	Salary competitiveness ratio	Salary offered by your company divided by salary offered by your competitors.
Employee	Time to hire	Elapsed time between job posting and first day on the job.
Corporate and social responsibility	Energy consumption	Amount of energy consumed in a given period.
Corporate and social responsibility	Savings level due to conservation	Hard dollar savings from conservation efforts.
Corporate and social responsibility	Volunteer hours	Number of hours employees volunteer their time (to organizations or individuals).
Corporate and social responsibility	Donations	Dollars donated to charitable organizations or causes.

■ DON'T TRACK EVERYTHING

Keep in mind that the list of KPIs provided is for reference only. There are advocates for tracking everything you possibly can, which may result in dozens or hundreds of KPIs. I am not one of those advocates and am a proud alumnus of Less Is More University. Go LIMU! Home of the Fighting Minimalists!

In sports, we track so many performance indicators, or stats, that it can be mind-boggling. But it is a graduated level of tracking. We would be out of our minds to track all of the same stats for a peewee league baseball team as are tracked for a major league baseball team. If we did, we would simply have no time left to manage all of those unruly parents in the stands. You know who I'm talking about.

The same is true in business. A small business can't possibly track the same amount of performance indicators as a large one can, nor should it try.

In the next chapter, we will discuss pairing KPIs in order to track the cause and effect that various KPIs have on one another. But for now, just think about and identify a few metrics that hold meaning for you. You might identify at least one from each of the six categories. You might establish a rule of thumb that you won't have more than three from any category. You might want to create a list of your own, or perhaps only track industry-specific metrics. For example, if you are a dentist, you might track the number of active patients (versus the number of patients on the book). If you are a software developer, you might track the number of bugs (errors) per release.

Do whatever feels right for you and your organization, but don't go overboard. Properly tracking metrics can be time-consuming. Large companies have entire teams dedicated to nothing else. Small and medium-sized businesses simply can't dedicate that much time and resources to it, so whatever your list ultimately includes, be sure to take that into consideration.

Bob Frost identifies a method for assessing whether specific metrics are right for you. He suggests asking a series of questions and rating the response from one to four, with one being "no value" and four being "extremely valuable." Sum it up. At certain score levels, you are advised whether you have the right metric or not.

You don't have to go through a process as elaborate as that, but if your gut instincts aren't telling you what to measure, then Frost's process is worth looking into.

Start with the end in mind and work backward from there.

As my leadership team and I began our journey toward building the company to $50 million and beyond, we had specific KPIs in mind, right from the start. We added more as we became smarter and as our plan progressed. This was particularly true of operational performance measurements.

In our business, we catered to federally defined programs that were delivered either at the state level or through the private sector. These were service-oriented contracts, with the service enabled by software that we developed. In most cases, minimal service level agreements, or SLAs, were defined by the government or the clients with whom we held contracts.

In simple terms, an SLA is a pledge or requirement to deliver given services within defined parameters, often time and quality based. For example, an SLA might be to pay an insurance claim within a certain number of days of when the loss is first reported, or it might be a requirement to answer the phone in a call center within a certain number of seconds.

Most of the time, our contracts included five to eight SLAs. Fortunately, we never came across a client who insisted on an unreasonably long laundry list of SLAs. But it helped that we had already defined them for ourselves and that our expectations were typically more aggressive than those of our customers.

Some people call this the "underpromise and overdeliver" method. I don't like that term because it sounds as if you're telling a lie. I prefer to instead think of it as signing up to deliver what is expected of you, then shooting to go above and beyond expectations.

Our SLAs gave us a built-in framework from which to measure operational performance, which in turn provided us with logical employee performance measurements, which in turn formed the basis for our pay-for-performance and bonus plans. All of this fed customer and employee satisfaction, which ultimately improved our sales and financial performance.

By default, we worked our way backward from the end state. The SLAs were defined. We knew what we had to do. Working backward, we had to figure out how we would do it. This is a theme repeated throughout this book. Don't worry about "how," initially. Worry about "what." Figure out how later. President John F. Kennedy probably provides us with the most famous example of this when he declared that by the end of the decade (the

1960s), we would safely send a man to the moon and back. He had no idea how we would do it when he made that proclamation, just that we would.

■ DON'T BE AFRAID TO THINK BIG

You hear advice all the time about starting small and thinking big, or thinking big and starting small. Some people even say think big and start big or start small and think small. It's all so confusing, and it seems like we just can't get a consensus. It also can be somewhat offensive because "big" is in the eyes of the beholder. So I say, take a leap of faith and go for it. Go big, whatever "big" means to you, and ignore the critics.

We used to say, "Go big or go home!" in our quest to grow the company. One of the members of the leadership team frequently used to say, "If we aren't growing, we're dying," while another often said, "We didn't come all this way to lay up!" That kind of spirit was necessary if we were going to make it, and it caught on.

True, we weren't a huge multibillion-dollar enterprise, but $50 million in annual revenue was pretty big in our world, so we thought big. Again, starting with the end in mind, we would have to do some pretty big things to get there.

So we developed big, nonoperational objectives right up front:

· Penetrate one of our defined markets with a new service within twelve months and reach 35 percent market share within the next three years (the market was established and mature, and this task would not be easy, but we felt we had a market disrupter in our tool belt).

· Dominate two of our defined markets by obtaining a greater than 50 percent share of each within two years (we were already a major player in each of these mature markets, but had been losing significant market share during the previous three years and were no longer the leader in either).

We didn't just make up these objectives willy-nilly. There was rhyme and reason to our big objectives. They were big because they had to be. Without objectives like these, there was no clear or reasonable path toward reaching $50 million. So starting with the end in mind, we worked our way backward to determine how much opportunity there was for us to win new business in our defined niche markets, and whether or not that would legitimately get us to our goal. By going through this exercise, we determined that we had to dominate two of our markets and we had to penetrate at least one new market.

Without doing that, we would not reach $50 million. Once the big objectives were logically defined, it became a simpler task to break them down into more manageable KPIs that supported the objectives that supported the vision.

■ THE CHAPTER 7 WRAP

In this chapter, we discussed the importance of metrics:

· They help keep us honest,

·   They help us understand how we are doing and where improvements have to be made, and

·   They help us focus on what is important to us.

Using Bernard Marr's book *Key Performance Indicators* as a basis, this chapter provided you with a list of several KPIS to consider, categorized by Marr's "perspectives," which fit neatly within the Business Is ART framework.

But I caution you not to identify too many metrics, especially if you are a small or medium-sized business, because doing so will take away precious resources you need to run the business. Find the metrics that have the most meaning to you.

Bob Frost's book *Measuring Performance* offers a process for determining whether a KPI is meaningful to you if you are having trouble determining this for yourself.

In this chapter, we also provided you with the real-life example of how we determined KPIS by working backward from client and industry requirements and from our vision. Start with the end in mind.

In the next chapter, we will discuss pairing metrics to track cause and effect.

Before proceeding, please answer the following questions:

1.   Do you have any formal KPIS?
2.   If so, how many?
3.   If not, why not?
4.   Do you measure the right KPIS for your business?

EIGHT

CORRELATING METRICS

An interesting thing about book groups, it seems to me, is that there is no correlation between a brilliant book and a brilliant discussion. The first seems sometimes even to undermine the second.

STACY SCHIFF, PULITZER PRIZE—WINNING
AMERICAN NONFICTION AUTHOR

Curse you, Stacy Schiff and your Pulitzerized opinion! I want book groups everywhere reading and reviewing my book, discussing the ingenuity and brilliance of the twelve steps to approaching business as ART, and, at the very least, the aesthetic appeal of the Ping Chart! (See chapter 9.)

And so, undeterred by your haughty sentiment, I press on. "Correlation" represents the mutual relation between multiple things. We consciously and unconsciously correlate things all of the time in our everyday lives. For example, in cities we correlate certain times of day with heavy traffic, and we may therefore think of 8:00 a.m. to 9:30 a.m. as a bad time of day to drive.

But "correlation" should not be confused with "cause." We correlate the time of day with heavy traffic, but the time of day does not the cause the traffic. The simultaneous rush to get somewhere at a given time of day is the reason for it, and our standard work schedule is the root cause for that. We call this time of day "rush hour," but when I was in college, my friends called "Rush hour" that time of day when they gathered around the stereo and played the album *2112*, debating the evils and virtues of the priests of the "Temples of Syrinx."

I grew up in a farming community, where "rush hour" is a season, usually spring when farmers are planting or fall when they are harvesting. It is during these times of year you are most likely to get behind a slow-moving piece of farm equipment, causing traffic to sometimes back up as many as four or five cars deep. Frustrating!

But the point is this: "The Spirit of Radio" is my favorite Rush song. Why do I mention this now? Because I personally correlate traffic jams with listening to jams on the radio, which lifts my spirits and keeps me from going into road rage mode.

Aha! Full circle: which might make an excellent title for the next Rush album.

Correlation should also not be confused with coordination. We coordinate things like throw pillows for the couch, shoes with a suit, solids with stripes, wall color with trim and accent colors, and white wine with fish. We often refer to this as "pairing," which will be discussed later in this chapter, but it is not the same as correlation.

In business, we often overlook correlation because while we think of it in everyday simple, informal terms, when we attempt to formalize it, our inner statistics professor begins to whisper in our ears, saying things like this:

> *Intuitively, the relationship is "strong" if the points in a scatterplot cluster tightly around some straight line. If this straight line rises from left to right, then the relationship is positive and the measurements are positive numbers. If it falls from left to right, then the relationship is negative and the measures are negative numbers.*
>
> FROM *DATA ANALYSIS AND DECISION MAKING WITH MICROSOFT EXCEL*, BY ALBRIGHT, WINSTON, AND ZAPPE[1]

Indeed! But might this also lead us to say, "the limitation of covariance as a descriptive measure is that it is affected by the units in which X and Y are measured"? Yes! Indeed, it very well might.

If you understood little of the previous statements, I have successfully made my point: it doesn't have to be so complicated.

■ CAUSE AND EFFECT

> *Shallow men believe in luck or in circumstance. Strong men believe in cause and effect.*
>
> RALPH WALDO EMERSON, AMERICAN AUTHOR

---

1   S. Christian Albright, Wayne L. Winston, and Christopher Zappe, *Data Analysis and Decision Making with Microsoft Excel* (Pacific Grove, California: Duxbury Press, 1999).

Complicated statistics and equations certainly have their value, and they are absolutely necessary in science-related fields. Additionally, politicians and pundits rely quite heavily on complicated statistics and equations to manipulate the numbers to provide evidence for whatever policies they subscribe to (insert smiley face here).

But to maximize success in running a small to medium-sized business—all apologies and due respect to my Executive MBA faculty and staff at the Ohio State University—it just isn't feasible or necessary to dive that deeply into statistical analysis.

However, I don't think any of us want to go up against Mr. Emerson, so let's run with his theory on cause, effect, and the shallow man for a bit.

Cause and effect is different from correlation because while correlation describes how we relate one thing to another, cause and effect refers to the actual impact one thing has on another.

Going back to our $50 million example, the former executive who decided the client did not need a web-based solution made a correlation between technology and function, causing him to conclude that the change in technology itself would offer no real value to the client by way of improved functionality. The effect of this decision was to lose market share to competitors that were willing to move toward a web-based strategy.

There is an entire field of study based on cause and effect analysis, made popular by Professor Kaoru Ishikawa, who is widely viewed as a pioneer in the subject of quality management. In his 1989 book entitled *Introduction to Quality Control*, Ishikawa defines a technique that is commonly referred to as "fishbone diagrams" wherein the completed diagram looks a bit like the skeleton of a fish. The fishbone diagram process largely goes like this:

1. Identify the problem.
2. Identify major factors contributing to the problem.
3. Identify potential causes.
4. Analyze the diagram to zero in on root causes.

Cause and effect analysis is a smart thing to do, particularly when you are looking for ways to improve or control quality. But for running a small to medium-sized business, again, something like fishbone diagrams and formal cause and effect techniques may be overkill unless you are skilled in the art of "filleting"—a made-up term thrown in here to say, "use these diagrams and techniques, but don't go overboard."

And yet, you should not ignore cause and effect any more than you should ignore correlation. Business Is ART therefore recommends that when you track KPIs, or performance metrics, you don't look at them on their own, but instead pair them with others so that you can note correlations and cause and effect, ultimately providing you with a more complete picture of the true health of your business.

■ PAIRING THEORY

I have observed that we too often ignore correlation and cause and effect in business by viewing performance metrics one at a time. For example, in our business plan we might identify four major indicators by which we measure the success of this year's business performance, as follows:

1. Revenue
2. Profit
3. Customer satisfaction
4. Employee satisfaction

These are all good things to identify as key performance indicators and for which to set targeted objectives. But if we measure each one in a vacuum, we are not seeing a complete picture. A more effective means of viewing them, without overcomplicating things, is to look at pairs of metrics that are correlated, or that affect one another.

The pairing of business performance metrics is as much of a science and an art form as pairing wine with food. Now remember, one of the basic premises of Business Is ART is that we want to keep things as simple as possible, because the small to medium-sized business leader doesn't have the time and resources to do more than that.

Therefore, in pairing performance metrics, we are looking more for the "white wine goes with fish" approach than the "Grüner Veltliner goes with dishes that have lots of fresh herbs" approach.

In an article about pairing beer with food, beer expert Garrett Oliver discusses the "flavor hook...the part of the beer's flavor and aroma that matches, harmonizes or accentuates the flavors in your food. When the flavors meet on your tongue, they 'recognize' each other and this creates a harmony."[2]

He discusses, as an example, the caramel flavors that develop in grilled and roasted foods (e.g., grilled meats or caramelized onions), arguing that they are best paired with beers that have a caramel accent.

To bring this food example to bear on my point here, I might subscribe to the "Cold beer tastes pretty good with a cheeseburger" school of pairing theory. In this same school, I might add, "But it doesn't taste good with a cream-filled doughnut."

The level of complexity recommended in the Business Is ART pairing of performance metrics is not much more complicated than that. It's important to recognize and track correlation and cause and effect by pairing metrics, but we don't want the process to be so complicated that it is infeasible, and hence, doesn't get done. We want our donuts glazed, not our eyes. And by the way, an IPA or a nut brown ale is said to pair well with a plain, glazed donut.

All of this said, you don't have to apply pairing theory to your metrics to be successful. In the $50 million example, we never consciously or unconsciously looked at pairing. In doing the research for this book, I went back over the original and subsequent plans we put together to achieve our $50 million goal and never found any reference to applying anything like pairing theory. But I have to wonder, if we had, would we have been even more successful?

---

2 Garrett Oliver, "Matching Beer and Food at the Brewmaster's Table," *All About Beer* 24 July 1, 2003, http://allaboutbeer.com/article/matching-beer-food-at-the-brewmasters-table.

Now, let's turn our attention to some recommendations on the pairing of some of the KPIs identified in the previous chapter. Fair warning: the rest of this chapter may seem a little complex at times, but bear with me. We'll bring it all together and make sense of it. I know what you're thinking right now: no way does beer taste good with donuts.

■ KPI PAIRING RECOMMENDATIONS

Again, one of the points to Business Is ART is to keep things simple. At first glance, this is where things might seem to go off the rails. But the qualifier here is that the following section attempts to provide you with multiple options for your consideration. I am not—I repeat, not—recommending that you use all of them, most of them, or even a lot of them. In fact, please don't. This is also not an exhaustive list of possible pairings; in fact, please define your own additional KPIs.

Recall from the previous chapter that we have identified and defined a number of potential KPIs for your consideration and that these KPIs fall into one of six categories as follows:

- Financial
- Customer
- Sales and marketing
- Operational
- Employee
- Social responsibility

The methodology applied to creating recommended pairings of the KPIs is fairly simple. First, each KPI from a specific category is paired with another KPI from the same category. Second, each KPI in a specific category is paired with one KPI from each of the other categories. The pairings are recommendations based on my experience and opinion. You do not have to follow these recommendations at all. They are merely provided to give you a starting point.

For example, in the table that follows, I paired "profit" with each of the following: revenue growth rate, net promoter score, new accounts/customers, Six Sigma level, employee satisfaction, and energy consumption for reasons that are explained in more detail later. I paired them this way to suggest that for your business, any one or more of these particular pairings *might* make sense for you. If so, run with it. If not, ignore it.

Reading the table is much more simple than it may appear at first glance. Don't be overwhelmed. Column titles in the table are as follows:

# = The KPI number assigned to the KPI, based on its order of presentation in the table
F = Financial category
C = Customer category
SM = Sales and marketing category
O = Operational category
E = Employee category
SR = Social responsibility category

There is no significance to the numbering scheme in the "#" column. It just represents the order in which the KPI happened to fall on the table and is simply a means of identifying each KPI numerically. It does not denote an order of importance.

Here are a couple of examples to help you read the table. In the second row of the table, the first KPI listed (one) is in the financial category. The KPI is net profit. It pairs nicely with KPI eight, which is revenue growth rate, also from the financial category (F). It also pairs nicely with KPI fourteen, net promoter score, from the customer category (C). Read the other rows and columns similarly.

TABLE 8.1. KEY PERFORMANCE INDICATOR PAIRINGS.

#	CATEGORY	KPI	F	C	SM	O	E	SR
1	Financial	Net profit	8	14	21	27	42	48
2	Financial	Net profit margin	8	16	22	27	42	48
3	Financial	Gross profit	8	17	21	34	41	50
4	Financial	Gross profit margin	8	17	22	34	41	50
5	Financial	Operating profit	8	17	21	27	41	51
6	Financial	Operating profit margin	8	17	22	27	41	51
7	Financial	EBITDA	1	14	20	27	40	48
8	Financial	Revenue growth rate	1	17	21	30	41	50
9	Financial	Return on investment	8	16	20	28	40	49
10	Financial	Debt to equity ratio	8	15	20	31	44	48
11	Financial	Cash on hand	12	17	22	35	42	48
12	Financial	Average accounts receivable	11	17	21	32	47	50

#	CATEGORY	KPI	F	C	SM	O	E	SR
13	Financial	Accounts receivable turn-over ratio	11	17	20	32	47	50
14	Customer	Net promoter score	8	18	21	30	43	50
15	Customer	Customer retention rate	1	16	20	30	44	50
16	Customer	Customer satisfaction index	2	17	20	30	42	50
17	Customer	Customer turnover rate	2	18	20	35	45	50
18	Customer	Customer complaints	4	16	20	35	45	50
19	Sales and marketing	Market growth rate	8	14	20	27	43	50
20	Sales and marketing	Market share	8	15	21	30	42	50
21	Sales and marketing	New accounts/customers	8	14	22	35	43	50
22	Sales and marketing	Cost per lead	5	14	23	37	44	51
23	Sales and marketing	Search engine rankings	8	14	24	30	43	50
24	Sales and marketing	Click through rate	8	14	25	30	43	50
25	Sales and marketing	Page views	8	14	26	30	43	50
26	Sales and marketing	Bounce rates	8	14	21	30	43	50
27	Operational	Six Sigma level	6	18	22	35	42	49
28	Operational	Capacity use rate	4	16	22	36	44	48
29	Operational	Order fulfillment cycle time	3	16	21	38	45	50
30	Operational	Delivery in full, on time rate	3	16	21	38	42	50
31	Operational	Inventory shrinkage rate	7	18	21	27	40	48
32	Operational	Project schedule variance	3	16	21	38	42	50

#	CATEGORY	KPI	F	C	SM	O	E	SR
33	Operational	Project cost variance	4	16	21	38	42	50
34	Operational	Rework level	4	16	21	35	42	50
35	Operational	Quality	1	16	21	27	42	50
36	Operational	Equipment availability	6	16	21	37	44	48
37	Operational	Equipment performance	6	16	21	36	45	48
38	Operational	Overall equipment effectiveness	6	16	21	27	42	48
39	Operational	First contact resolution	5	18	21	27	43	50
40	Employee	Human capital value added	8	18	20	27	41	50
41	Employee	Revenue per employee	1	18	21	29	42	51
42	Employee	Employee satisfaction index	4	17	21	35	43	50
43	Employee	Staff advocacy score	1	14	22	39	44	51
44	Employee	Employee churn rate	4	17	22	30	45	50
45	Employee	Average employee tenure	4	18	22	30	46	50
46	Employee	Salary competitiveness ratio	6	18	22	35	47	51
47	Employee	Time to hire	4	18	21	29	46	50
48	Corporate and social responsibility	Energy consumption	1	14	23	28	40	49
49	Corporate and social responsibility	Savings level due to conservation	1	16	23	27	43	48
50	Corporate and social responsibility	Volunteer hours	2	16	23	35	42	51
51	Corporate and social responsibility	Donations	8	16	23	35	43	50

Now let's discuss a few of these that, again, in my opinion, are the most critical and sensible. We'll limit the discussion to one KPI from within each of the first five of the six categories, just to give you an idea of the thought processes behind some of the recommended pairings.

There is no right or wrong to this. Just as in pairing wine or beer with food, there is a mix of science and art to it. A significant amount of the art boils down to taste. What "tastes" right to you?

So that I don't have to keep retyping the word "recommendation," please keep in mind that's all these are: recommendations.

Net Profit Pairs Nicely with...
Starting with the financial category, let's pick on net profit because, at the end of the day, one of the most telling indicators of success in business, even for nonprofit business, is net profit. How much is left over after all expenses have been taken into consideration?

Within the financial category, net profit is paired with revenue growth rate for some obvious reasons and for some not-so-obvious reasons. One of the obvious reasons is that you should be interested in knowing how new sales are affecting your bottom line. For example, if the bottom line is going down or not moving even though sales are up, it may indicate that expenses are getting out of hand. Alternatively, it could be indicative of a selling price point that is too low to be profitable.

There are any number of things this could be telling you, including, "Stop selling that product or service!"

A not-so-obvious reason for this pairing is that companies and managers sometimes hide or fail to see the true health of their business, artificially pumping up the profits by cutting expenses to ridiculously low levels when sales growth is flat or in decline. If you correlate the two and monitor their cause and effect, you can see a more complete picture of what is really going on inside your business or organization.

One of the most frustrating experiences I have ever had with this happened a few years after we had met the $50 million challenge, when we were acquired by a large publicly traded company. We were profitable beyond the estimated "sold margin" (the margin at which we expected to perform based on selling price and estimated cost to deliver). We were well above company average in profitability. But the division under which we were ultimately organized had some business units that were struggling. Rather than focus on improving the struggling units, management expected the other units to pick up the slack by cutting expenses. It was a complete "one-for-all and all-for-one" approach, which works nicely in movies but not in the real world.

Eventually, we were squeezed so hard that we could no longer provide good service to our customers. We began to lose clients as well as margin. The more margin we lost, the more we were squeezed. Had someone at the decision-making level seen the cause and effect, they might have realized how damaging the cost-cutting measures had become.

Outside the financial category, net profit is paired with net promoter score from the customer category, new accounts/customers from the sales and marketing category, Six Sigma level from the operational category, employee satisfaction index from the employee category, and energy consumption from the social responsibility category.

Profit in business comes from repeat customers, customers that boast about your project or service, and that bring friends with them.
W. EDWARDS DEMING, AMERICAN ENGINEER, STATISTICIAN, PROFESSOR, AUTHOR, LECTURER, AND MANAGEMENT CONSULTANT

Net profit is paired with net promoter score because it is useful to know if and how your profit is affected when you have customers who promote your goods and services, versus those who will tell anyone listening that your products and services stink, or those who just don't say anything at all. This will give you a pretty clear indication of how much work you need to do to not just bring satisfaction up but get customers talking about you in a positive light.

It's paired with the new accounts/customers KPI for some of the same reasons it is paired with revenue growth rate. It is important to know whether new sales are increasing profits, and it is important to know whether a lack of new sales has affected revenue growth at all. Armed with this information, you can then make better-informed decisions about how and where to set your marketing venues and budget.

Net profit is paired with Six Sigma level because undertaking Six Sigma initiatives is not free. Six Sigma takes resources, which cost money. And while the intent of Six Sigma isn't solely to improve your bottom line, it sure is nice to know it did. So if you have achieved a Six Sigma level of "über, super, duper, can't get any more six than this sigma" status, but have gained nothing on the bottom line, you have to ask questions like "Why not? Is it worth it? Are we focused on the right things?" And then take appropriate action.

Net profit is paired with employee satisfaction index because it is far too easy to forget about or ignore what impact employee satisfaction has on the bottom line. If you see employee satisfaction going down while profits are going up, it could indicate a number of things, including that employees are being overworked or underpaid. If employee satisfaction is high, but profits are low, it could be a sign that policies and corporate culture are too relaxed and carefree. In either case, the business model is not sustainable over the long haul, and corrective action is needed.

Net profit is paired with social responsibility because studies increasingly find that formal social responsibility programs improve the sustainability of the business model over the long haul. If your program includes initiatives to cut energy consumption, the "feel-good" part of you is happy to know you reduced your business's carbon footprint. But the businessperson in you also wants to know how that contributes to the bottom line.

It is important to note here that social responsibility programs and initiatives do not always have to have a directly measurable effect on the bottom line. It is also important to note that you should not define your social responsibility program based on the directly measurable effect on the bottom line. Define programs that are consistent with who you are and with your company culture first. Then ask if they will affect the bottom line. If so, great. Measure it. If not, great. Feel good about it.

Customer Retention Rate Pairs Nicely with...

> *The well-satisfied customer will bring*
> *the repeat sale that counts.*
>
> JAMES CASH PENNEY, FOUNDER OF J.C. PENNEY

From the customer category, customer retention has been singled out because the best way to grow a business is by creating a solid customer base. As Penney points out, they will be back to buy even more.

This KPI pairs nicely with the customer satisfaction index from the same category. If retention is high but satisfaction is low, it could be telling you that your market is ripe for a competitor to disrupt things, potentially driving you out of business. Right now, your customers are only with you because they don't have another choice.

This was precisely the situation in our $50 million challenge. At the time, there was arguably only one competitor that stood in our way of completely disrupting and grabbing a large percentage of one of the markets we served. The clear market leader had very low customer satisfaction but a virtual monopoly, so their retention rate was very high. And then we came along. We had a clearly superior technical solution, absolutely no experience delivering the associated business service, and a promise to do better than the other guy. The client was so miserable that they were ready to take a chance on us. We won the deal and turned the struggling $1 million business sector into a $6 million business sector, planting the seeds for additional growth that would eventually increase almost tenfold.

The competitor lost sight of customer satisfaction, while continuing to feel good about retention. The result: they were caught completely by surprise at our sudden emergence in the market.

Conversely, if retention is low but satisfaction is high, it could mean you need to diversify your products and services so that the customer has something to come back to. Unless your product is meant to be a "one and done" thing, never to be bought again, like the fictional car that will last forever, something is not right with your business model.

Outside the customer category, this KPI pairs nicely with net profit from the financial category, market share from the sales and marketing category, delivery in full, on-time rate from the operational category, employee churn rate from the employee category, and volunteer hours from the social responsibility category.

Customer retention pairs nicely with net profit for some very obvious reasons, but since we already discussed net profit, let's move on to the next pairing: market share. When customer retention and market share are viewed in tandem, an interesting picture begins to emerge. For example, if retention is high but market share is low, it isn't necessarily a bad thing, but it could be telling you any number of things: maybe the market is again ripe for a disruptor because no one has incentive to move, or perhaps you are at risk of losing customers who have been loyal to you for a long time. On the other hand, if your market share is high but retention is low, it may be an indicator that the market is growing and you are growing with it because of new sales outpacing the loss of existing customers, but once market growth slows or stagnates, you will have some serious trouble.

Customer retention pairs nicely with delivery in full, on-time rate because you may find that retention increases if you can make a few tweaks to improve your delivery rate.

Customer retention pairs nicely with employee churn rate because you may discover that the same things that drive customers away also drive employees away (or lead both to stay). You may find that a high employee churn rate actually causes low customer retention. Your staff might be leaving because they see that your business is unable to keep customers. If your customer retention rate is low and employee churn rate is also low, it may be telling you that you are keeping the wrong people (or skills).

Finally, customer retention pairs well with volunteer hours because if customers see you and your employees are doing volunteer work, especially for a cause they believe in, it may tip the scales in your favor if you are otherwise in a dead heat with a competitor for that client's business. It may also show that your staff is receiving valuable experience through their volunteer efforts that improves customer satisfaction and therefore retention.

Again, the effect on the bottom line shouldn't be the driving force behind your social responsibility program, but it very well can be further justification for the program. At the very least, you should understand how your social responsibility programs affect the bottom line.

Market Share Pairs Well with...

> *It's not about market share. If you have a successful company, you will get your market share. But to get a successful company, what do you have to have? The same metrics of success that your customer does.*
> GORDON BETHUNE, FORMER CEO OF
> CONTINENTAL AIRLINES

It should be noted that Continental no longer exists. It was acquired. But that all came after Mr. Bethune's retirement, so let's give the guy the benefit of the doubt and go with his quote. I like it because it helps drive home the importance of how you define success and the metrics that help you determine how successful you are. It also drives home an important reason for pairing KPIs: that if you only look at each KPI individually, you will miss the big picture. Simply picking a market share target at random and then doing everything you can to achieve that target is foolish and shortsighted. What should be important is how other things you are doing are affecting market share.

So market share as a KPI pairs well with new accounts/ customers from the same category of sales and marketing. Outside that category, it also pairs well with revenue growth rate from the financial category, customer retention from the customer category, quality from the operational category, employee satisfaction index from the employee category, and volunteer hours from the social responsibility category.

Revenue growth rate is perhaps the most obvious combination with market share. Suppose this year you capture the majority of a market but your revenue growth rate is down, flat, or not climbing on par with your market share growth rate. One possible reason is that you effectively "bought" the increased market share by setting prices that were too low to be sustainable. An additional consequence may be decreased satisfaction among clients who find out you sold to someone else at bargain basement prices while they had to pay full price. The practice may cause once-loyal customers to rethink their loyalty. If this were the case, simply feeling great about market share could lead to a collapse of your business.

Likewise, suppose you invested very heavily to produce a widget of unbeatable quality, but your market share didn't improve. That may be a sign that the market perceives no value in additional quality. Even if it is a false perception, perception becomes reality. In this case, you can either lower quality or step up your marketing game so that customers value the additional quality.

Employee satisfaction index and volunteer hours have already been discussed as they relate to other KPIs.

We will skip them relative to market share because the reasoning is very similar.

Quality Pairs Well with...

> *Quality is not an act, it is a habit.*
>
> ARISTOTLE

Quality pairs so well with so many things that it is hard to limit it to a few. It's kind of the house red at a restaurant that specializes in steak, and the house white at a seafood restaurant. It's the Bud Light on tap at Buffalo Wild Wings; it goes with everything on the menu.

But as mentioned before, quality, when measured by itself, tells you almost nothing beyond how high the quality is. Quality pairs well with Six Sigma level within the operational category, which may even be a little redundant since one objective of Six Sigma is to improve quality. Outside of this category, quality pairs well with net profit from the financial category, customer satisfaction from the customer category, new accounts/customers from the sales and marketing category, employee satisfaction from the employee category, and volunteer hours from the social responsibility category.

There has already been some discussion of all of these paired KPIs, but one thing that might not be so obvious is how quality correlates with volunteer hours. It's actually pretty simple. Typically, volunteer hours help employees feel good about themselves. When they feel good about themselves, they tend to perform better (in both productivity and quality) at work. Pairing the two may help you understand the interaction between volunteer hours and quality; how much is enough and how much is too much?

Employee Satisfaction Pairs Well with...
Many will argue that employee satisfaction is important but not as important as employee engagement, and I would tend to agree. After all, you can have a very satisfied employee who is not engaged and therefore not really productive. In that case, satisfaction is relatively meaningless.

But I left employee engagement out of the Business Is ART framework for a few reasons. One, the KPIs included here are merely suggestions and not a definitive list. If you want to include employee engagement, by all means do it.

Second, employee engagement is derived from a series of questions surveyed from the employee, as opposed to a yes or no answer or a mathematical formula. This makes it a bit complex to understand, and one of the goals of Business Is ART is to make things simple for you. And finally, these surveys can be expensive.

That said, I do believe employee engagement is more telling than employee satisfaction, and I encourage those with the means to use it as a KPI to do so. But in its absence, you can estimate employee engagement by looking at some of the other KPIs included in the recommended list.

With that in mind, employee satisfaction pairs well with revenue per employee from within the same category. Outside the employee category, it pairs well with gross profit margin from the financial category, customer turnover rate from the customer category, new accounts/customers from the sales and marketing category, quality from the operational category, and volunteer hours from the social responsibility category. Again, you can use this collection of pairings to derive employee engagement for yourself without additional surveys and expense.

This may seem a bit overwhelming, but please don't let it be. The old phrase "there are many ways to skin a cat" applies here. There are in fact many ways to measure success, but don't try to employ all of them. This is all we are trying to say:

- Identify some KPIs that are important to you and your business
- Limit that to a few (four to twelve)
- Consider pairing each KPI with another to get a more complete view
- Consider this list as no more than a sampling of the many possibilities, and do what is best for you

■ THE CHAPTER 8 WRAP

In this chapter, we learned that my friends are middle-aged nerds who still go to Rush concerts. Perhaps more importantly, we defined the word "correlation" and discussed how it is different from cause and effect. Both need to be taken into consideration when determining and reporting on key performance indicators (metrics).

When KPIs are observed on their own, they don't tell the whole tale, and you may be missing the point. For example, boasting about capturing the lion's share of the market is meaningless if, in so doing, your revenue growth rate fell to zero, which could show that you gave away the products and services just to be able to say, "We are the market leader."

A better way to look at KPIs is by pairing them with other KPIs where there is a correlation or a cause and effect that is of interest to you. This interest may be important to the bottom line, or it may simply be an experiment or something you want to observe out of sheer curiosity. There is no right or wrong pairing, and just as in pairing wine or beer with food, it often comes down to individual taste. What tastes good to you? That is to say, what makes sense to you and your business?

Finally, this chapter provides you with an extensive list of possible KPIs and recommended pairings of each. It discusses the logic behind these pairings, but again, these are recommendations. Do what makes sense for you.

In the next chapter, we will show you a method called the Ping Chart for tracking paired metrics.

Before proceeding, please answer the following questions:

1. Have you ever considered pairing performance metrics?
2. What KPIs would you pair together to provide a better view of the health of your business?

NINE

PING CHARTING

*Of all of our inventions for mass communication, pictures
still speak the most universally understood language.*

WALT DISNEY

The late actor Telly Savalas portrayed a lollipop-sucking
detective on the 1970s television series *Kojak*. Kojak
had two famous tag lines, the first being, "Who loves
ya, baby?" and the second being, "Everybody should
have a little Greek in them." It was the '70s. We won't
go there.

In the mid-70s, Savalas, rather infamously, recorded
a cover of the sappy song "If" by the band Bread. There
are multiple video versions of it out there, but the best
is the one in which he appears on *Disco*, a German television program, in an open-necked shirt, wearing gold
chains and lighting a cigarette before he thoughtfully
launches into the lyrics.

On the screen in the background is the face of a blonde woman trying to look like...I'm really not sure what she's trying to look like. To me, it's an expression that says, "Bitte beeilen Sie sich. Ich muss wirklich pinkeln." In English this means, "Please hurry. I really have to go to the bathroom."

"If" you have never seen Savalas's rendition of this classic song, you simply must stop what you are doing right now, find it on YouTube, sit back, and enjoy the ride.

Now that you have returned, let's continue. The song includes the lyrics, "If a picture paints a thousand words, then why can't I paint you?"

Romantic, yes? Forget about it. Things aren't that complicated. At least, they don't need to be. The "simplification" industry is another one that sells thousands, perhaps millions, of books, seminars, workshops, methodologies, and software every year. Quite frankly, this book and its accompanying software is now among them (the defendant pleads "guilty," Your Honor).

Confucius is sometimes credited with saying, "Life is really simple, but we insist on making it complicated."

I did a simple search for books on simplifying life and received simply countless results. My favorite was perhaps the one entitled *100 Ways to Simplify Your Life*. Really? One hundred? Now I need a complex filing system to store and look up the hundred ways to simplify things?

We just make things too hard. Did you know that Michelangelo painted the Sistine Chapel primarily using just three colors: green, purple, and salmon? Neither did I, but I read it somewhere on the Internet and it fit my contention that "less is more," so I am presenting it here as fact. But if Michelangelo slipped in another color or two on his palette, that's OK. He still created arguably the greatest and most complex works of painted art ever, using some pretty simple tools. And so can you with your business.

■ PICTURES AND GRAPHS AND CHARTS, OH MY!

> *The greatest value of a picture*
> *is when it forces us to notice*
> *what we never expected to see.*
> JOHN TUKEY, AMERICAN MATHEMATICIAN

There are a multitude of methods for visualizing data in order to create information, and I don't know of a one-size-fits-all approach. Sometimes, as when pairing food with beer or wine, pairing metrics, or deciding which colors to put on your palette, determining how to graphically illustrate information comes down to personal taste. Sometimes it comes down to need or to what functions best for a given situation. For example, a pie chart might illustrate market share better than a bar chart would, just as the color salmon might make a better base for Michelangelo to create skin pigmentation than would green (no disrespect to space people intended).

The best information-bearing tools provide you with graphical means to visualize information. The key here is "information."

In the Matrix movie series, the character Neo can see beyond the vision, or illusion, and into the binary code, or numbers, and is therefore able to interpret reality. He manipulates the matrix to stop bullets and fly through the air. In the business world, it's the opposite. We have to look beyond the numbers to see the reality.

Some people can pull a reverse Neo (an Oen—pronounced "o-wen") and see the picture just by looking at and beyond the numbers. You can imagine Warren Buffett is the Oen playing opposite Keanu Reeves's Neo. He probably doesn't need a bunch of visuals to tell him anything.

But most of us aren't Oen or Neo. When we look at a spreadsheet full of data we think, "I wonder if there's any Coke left in the vending machine."

We just don't get it, and we just don't see it. As Walt Disney said, pictures are the "most universally understood language." And so if we turn that raw data into information by creating artful illustrations, we can more easily understand it.

But pictures and graphs and charts (oh, my) are not magic. They are simply tools, or colors on your palette, that you can use to create your work of art. The Business Is ART framework adds one more tool, one more color to your palette, the Ping Chart, as a means of tracking and visualizing KPIs or performance metrics.

■ THE ORIGINS OF THE PING CHART

Do you ever wake up and think to yourself, "That dream was crazy, but it gives me a good idea"?

That state of consciousness is called the "hypno-pompic state." If you look up its definition, simply reading it may move you toward a "hypnagogic state," which is the onset of sleep. According to Wikipedia, when you are coming out of rapid eye movement sleep (REM) and in a hypnopompic state, "some of the creative insights attributed to dreams actually happen in this moment."[1]

The Ping Chart was conceived while I was in a hypno-pompic state. I woke up dreaming about it. The Business Is ART framework was conceived with the end in mind: the Ping Chart. From this notion, I worked backward, eventually defining the twelve steps to approaching business as ART, this book, the templates, and ultimately, the accompanying software. This is appropriate because, as previous chapters have suggested, the best way to plan is to start with the end in mind, then work your way backward. We have the hypnopompic state to thank for that, plus I just like saying "hypnopompic."

Many famous works of art, scientific theories, and inventions came from dreams, such as Einstein's theory of relativity and Elias Howe's sewing machine. Here are a few more examples:

---

1   Wikipedia contributors, "Hypnopompic," *Wikipedia, The Free Encyclopedia*, http://en.wikipedia.org/w/index.php?title=Hypnopompic&oldid= 637490572 (accessed March 29, 2015).

- John Lennon's song "#9 Dream"
- Christopher Nolan's movie *Inception*
- Salvador Dalí's painting *The Persistence of Memory*
- Paul McCartney's inspiration for the song "Yesterday"
- Stephen King's novel *Dreamcatcher*

And now, again, thanks to the hypnopompic state, *Business Is ART* too can take its place among these notable works...and with that, I will stop saying "hypnopompic."

In previous chapters, we discussed a few ways to get the creative juices flowing, but one of them may simply be to pay attention to your dreams. Keep a notepad or some other kind of recording device on the nightstand so that when you wake up with the next best thing to hit the market since the invention of the market, you can capture it, apologize to the person sleeping next to you, roll back over, and go back to sleep, without forgetting it later.

■ FOUNDATIONS OF THE PING CHART

Remember how I said you shouldn't overcomplicate things? Well, I might have gone a little bit in that direction when I developed the Ping Chart, but the actual end result is pretty simple to create and use. Let's start with the complexity that helped found the Ping Chart itself. That foundation is a combination of the 4.0 grading scale in the U.S. education system and sonar (sound navigation ranging), along with some color-coding and an X–Y axis thrown in for good measure.

In the 4.0 grade point scale, averages are first calculated on a percentage basis from 0 to 100. That percentage score is then translated to a scale that goes from 0.0 (very bad) to 4.0 (very good). The percentage score is also associated with a letter grade and the letter grade is associated with a number on the 4.0 scale. It sounds complicated but is really pretty simple.

The table for this scale is as follows:

TABLE 9.1. CALCULATING A GRADE POINT.

LETTER GRADE	PERCENTAGE	GRADE POINT
A+	97–100	4.0
A	93–96	3.9
A-	90–92	3.7
B+	87–89	3.3
B	83–86	3.0
B-	80–82	2.7
C+	77–79	2.3
C	73–76	2.0
C-	70–72	1.7
D+	67–69	1.3
D	65–66	1.0
F	<65	0.0

A sonar screen looks like the following:

FIGURE 9.1. A SAMPLE SONAR READOUT. SONAR MAPS THE
DISTANCE AND LOCATION OF UNDERWATER OBJECTS.

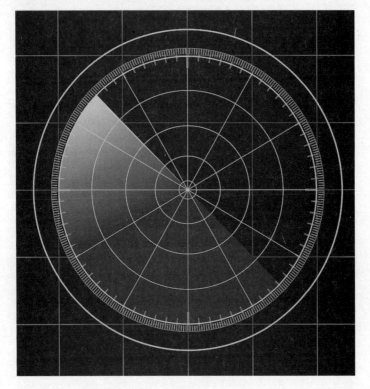

Basically, the sonar sends out a pulse of sound
(the ping) and then listens for an echo. The pings are
focused into a narrow beam that appears on the screen
as the long arm thingy, or LAT (technical term I just
made up). As the LAT swings around, it plots a point on
the sonar screen to show the direction and proximity of
every object it picks up. If you are in a submarine and
the ping of an enemy sub is really close to the center,

you should worry, because you may soon be dead. But, as you will see, in Ping Charting, dead center is right where you want to be.

Next, imagine you are laying an X–Y grid on top of the sonar, but this grid is different than most. It doesn't start with the coordinates (0,0). It starts with the center coordinates of (4,4). Now, using the points from the 4.0 scale and working backward (and outward), the points continue at 3.9, 3.7, 2.7, etc., all the way out to 0.

As a result of applying the X–Y grid, there are four quadrants on the chart, and this is where we really diverge from classic sonar. Each quadrant is a unique graph area for either a single KPI or a pair of KPIS. Each quadrant is where we will eventually plot a "ping" associated with that KPI or pair of KPIS.

But before we do, there are a couple more steps to creating the blank Ping Chart. First, going back to the 4.0 scale, we draw (or move) a series of circles on the chart, again with (4,4) as the center point. One circle each goes through the following points on the X–Y grid:

- 3.7
- 2.7
- 1.7
- 1.0
- 0.0

Now we add a little color. The circle that goes through the 3.7 points on the axis is green. The circle that goes through the 2.7 points on the axis is yellow. The circle that goes through the 1.7 points on the axis is red. The circle that goes through the 1.0 points on the axis is orange. And the circle that goes through the 0.0 points on the axis is black.

Now, we have the raw, devoid of data, empty Ping Chart, ready for plotting. Yes, it was one crazy dream.

■ PLOTTING THE PING CHART

We are almost ready to begin plotting the Ping Chart, but one more color scheme is applied before we do. It is consistent with the color scheme of the circles on the Ping Chart and is simply the application of color to the 4.0 scale as follows:

TABLE 9.2. COLOR SCHEME FOR THE PING CHART.

LETTER GRADE	PERCENTAGE	GRADE POINT	PING COLOR
A+	97–100	4.0	Blue
A	93–96	3.9	Green
A-	90–92	3.7	Green
B+	87–89	3.3	Yellow
B	83–86	3.0	Yellow
B-	80–82	2.7	Yellow
C+	77–79	2.3	Red

LETTER GRADE	PERCENTAGE	GRADE POINT	PING COLOR
C	73–76	2.0	Red
C-	70–72	1.7	Red
D+	67–69	1.3	Orange
D	65–66	1.0	Orange
F	<65	0.0	Black

For each quadrant, identify a single KPI or a pair of KPIs that you have defined as part of your strategic and business planning efforts. These are KPIs that you have determined are important to you for whatever the reason.

For illustrative purposes, let's suppose we identified the following KPIs during the planning process:

· Revenue growth rate
· Net profit
· Cash on hand
· Accounts receivable
· Market share
· New accounts/customers

Let's further suppose we would like to not just track these KPIs individually, but track most of them by pairing with others to visualize correlation or cause and effect. In this example, we have decided to track new accounts/customers as a singular KPI, but have paired the others as follows:

- Revenue growth and net profit
- Cash on hand and accounts receivable
- Revenue growth and market share

The single KPI, new accounts/customers, and the three paired KPIs provide us with four points we will plot on the Ping Chart (one in each quadrant).

During the planning process, we would have established targets for each of these KPIs. Throughout a given reporting period, we would have tracked our progress toward that KPI target (objective) and at the end of the reporting period, we would know how close we came to meeting it. For illustrative purposes, let's say we met them as follows:

- Revenue growth rate: met 90 percent of targeted growth rate
- Net profit: met 90 percent of net profit target
- Cash on hand: met 80 percent of cash on hand target
- Accounts receivable: met 70 percent of accounts receivable target
- Market share: met 80 percent of market share target
- New accounts/customers: met 75 percent of new accounts/customers target

The following table illustrates the resulting grade point score associated with each of the KPIs:

TABLE 9.3. GRADE POINT SCORES FOR A SAMPLE SET OF KPIS.

KPI	ACHIEVEMENT	GRADE POINT
Revenue growth rate	90%	3.7
Net profit	90%	3.7
Cash on hand	80%	2.7
Accounts receivable	70%	1.7
Market share	80%	2.7
New accounts/customers	75%	2.0

We are now ready to determine plot points for each of the quadrants in the Ping Chart. They are as follows:

TABLE 9.4. PLOTTING A SAMPLE SET OF KPIS ON THE PING CHART.

QUAD-RANT	KPI1	KPI1 GPA	KPI2	KPI2 GPA	PLOT COORDINATES
1	Revenue growth rate	3.7	Net profit	3.7	(3.7,3.7)
2	Cash on hand	2.7	Accounts receivable	1.7	(2.7,1.7)
3	Revenue growth rate	3.7	Market share	2.7	(3.7,2.7)
4	New accounts/customers	2.0	N/A	N/A	(2.0,2.0)

Sound complex? Maybe; especially for the guy who wrote the code for the software application. But all of this complexity leads to a very simple visual for how your business is doing.

Voilà! I give you…the Ping Chart:

FIGURE 9.2. A PING CHART SHOWING REVENUE GROWTH RATE PAIRED WITH NET PROFIT; CASH ON HAND PAIRED WITH ACCOUNTS RECEIVABLE; REVENUE GROWTH PAIRED WITH MARKET SHARE; AND NEW ACCOUNTS.

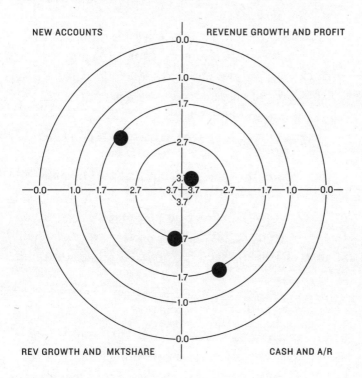

Using our example KPIs as pairings, we have created "pings" in each of the four quadrants of the Ping Chart based on the coordinates we determined in the previous table. We would then color-code those pings accordingly. If the ping fell within the center circle, it would be blue. If in the next, it would be green. Then yellow, red, orange, and black.

When all is said and done, all you have to do is:

1. Identify the KPIs that help you determine the success of your business.
2. Determine the targets (objectives) for those KPIs.
3. Determine which, if any, KPIs you will pair.
4. Track your progress toward achieving them.
5. Calculate the percentage that you actually achieved.
6. Plug it into the Ping Chart.
7. Create as many Ping Charts as you see fit.

Then comes the most fun, but perhaps the more difficult part. Pretty pictures are swell, but if you don't interpret them, they don't do you much good. If you stare at the *Mona Lisa* and all you walk away with is, "Old painting of woman," then you probably missed the point.

■ INTERPRETING THE PING CHART

So now you have this pretty picture that some may mistake for the target sheet from a shooting range (I assure you, good sirs and madams, that it is not), what do you do with it? First, you interpret its meaning. This may repeat some of the analysis of sample pairings from the previous chapter, but let's continue to use the KPIs and pairings used as examples in this chapter, and interpret the resulting Ping Chart.

Quadrant one pairs the revenue growth rate with profit. Ideally, as your revenue grows, you see your profit grow. In this example, they are both growing at not too bad a rate, right? A 3.7 is an A-. We should all want our kids to do so well in school. Because these two KPIS are growing in sync with one another, you may conclude that you have found a relatively good balance between the price the customer is willing to pay and the price that you need in order to be profitable (however you have defined it). You're in good shape here.

Quadrant two pairs cash on hand and accounts receivable. The news here is not quite so good. Cash on hand isn't too terrible. At a GPA of 2.7, that's a B-. It's nothing to ground your kid over. But accounts receivable doesn't look so great. It's a 1.7, which is a C-. That's OK for someone who just wants to graduate from high school, but isn't going to send the kid to the front of the line for college applications. It might be time to restrict phone and Internet access as well as take the keys to the car. That low score on accounts receivable is having a negative impact on cash. And while in this example you aren't doing too badly on cash, the poor performance of accounts receivable is having a direct negative impact on cash. Perhaps it is just enough to cause you to delay making a strategic purchase or repairing equipment. Perhaps you won't be able to fully make the next payroll. Perhaps it will force you to take out a loan or borrow against a line of credit when your sales told you that should not have been necessary. Any way you look at it, something will have to be done or the business will be at unnecessary risk.

Quadrant three pairs revenue growth with market share. We've already discussed that revenue growth looks pretty good. A-. But market share, while not too bad, is not as good. At 2.7, you are again at a B-. That's OK. Still respectable. Middle of the pack-ish, but not great. In this example, revenue growth that is outpacing market share growth could be indicative of a few things, depending on the market itself. It could be that inflation is a factor. Prices are going up, so revenue is increasing, but you aren't really getting a bigger slice of the pie. The pie itself (the market) might be growing, but your share of it is not growing as fast. Someone else is eating your lunch...which in this case is pie.

In quadrant four, we didn't pair new accounts/customers with anything, so we don't have any correlation or cause and effect that we are looking for or illustrating. In this example, we are simply saying we didn't do all that hot with selling to new clients. A 2.0 is a C average. Still passing, but the kid probably isn't headed to Harvard.

In this example, even though we didn't specifically pair anything with new accounts/customers, we might still note some correlation or cause and effect by looking at the entire Ping Chart because we can see that 1) our sales were not so hot, 2) our revenue growth was good, and 3) our market share growth was not so hot. From this we might interpret that we are doing a pretty good job of farming (selling within established accounts) but are weak in hunting (selling to new accounts).

We then have some decisions to make, starting with, "Is that OK?" From there, we ask more questions, make more decisions, and ultimately modify our plans accordingly.

▪ THE PURSUIT OF TRIVIA

In 1979, Canadians Chris Haney and Scott Abbott created the game *Trivial Pursuit*, which was first released in 1982 and quickly became a phenomenon that still delights and irritates bar patrons everywhere to this day.

We all know "that guy." Some of us are related to him. He's "that guy" that knows all of the answers, always has the highest score, and always gets a little irritated if the rest of us fail to stop our unrelated conversation when the next *Trivial Pursuit* question is asked and the clock starts ticking.

While the name "Trivial Pursuit" may have originated from a play on the word "trivia," which is what the game is all about, it has a dual meaning. "Trivial" is an adjective, meaning of little value or importance, which pretty much describes the point of *Trivial Pursuit*. It's the pursuit of information that has little value or importance. More succinctly, it's the pursuit of "that guy" to show the rest of us that he knows more information that has little value or importance than the rest of us.

All right, calm down, all of you gamers out there. Yes, there is value in fun, entertainment, the bringing together of people in social settings, and everything else you can say about the intrinsic value of *Trivial Pursuit*. But allow me to counter with this. The online news and entertainment company BuzzFeed published a list of twelve of the most difficult *Trivial Pursuit* questions of all time, which included, "Who was the official hair consultant to the 1984 Los Angeles Olympics?"

The follow-up question is, "So what?" So what if you know the answers to one, some, or all of the most difficult

Trivial Pursuit questions? The real question is, "What are you going to do with this information?"

At least in *Trivial Pursuit*, "that guy" can say, "Well, it's obvious what I am going to do with this information. I'm going to win this fricking game. That's what I'm going to do with this information, stupid."

Fair enough.

But outside of a game, information has to be actionable, or else it is merely the pursuit of trivia. Now that you understand something better, now that you have the information, now that you can visualize it, what are you going to do about it?

■ BUT I ALREADY DID MY PLAN!

Everyone has a plan 'til they get punched in the mouth.

MIKE TYSON, FORMER
HEAVYWEIGHT BOXING CHAMPION

Sometimes, seeing reality can be like a punch to the mouth. Once it's happened, we basically have four choices: crumple to the mat and wait to be counted out, just stand there and wait for the next one, turn and run, or quickly determine how to fight back. All of these are indeed plans, and any one of them might be the right one for that moment, with the probable exception of just standing there, waiting to take the next punch. Generally, that is not a good idea, and yet that is exactly what so many business leaders do.

We have the ability to create plans and define objectives. We have the ability to turn data into information.

We have the ability to interpret the information. And then, we turn into Al Pacino in the movie *Scarface*.

"I'm still standin', huh!"

Things didn't end well for Tony Montana, Pacino's character, shortly after shouting those words, and they won't end well for your business if that's the stance you choose to take when it's been punched in the mouth. Why would you just stand there? It goes back to things we discussed in the beginning of this book. Sometimes we don't want to admit mistakes, sometimes we just don't know what to do next, and ultimately, sometimes it's just too easy to do nothing.

But you have to do something in order to maximize success. Swallow a little pride, use the information you now have, and go back to adjust accordingly. Sometimes "doing something" might mean adjusting your strategy or your business plan. Sometimes it might mean changing your tactics or expectations. But it doesn't have to mean changing your vision. It can remain constant while everything else along the way changes rapidly.

All of this really is step twelve of the twelve-step method: Continually review, assess, refine, and modify the previous steps as necessary.

■ A WORD ON RESISTANCE TO CHANGE

Sometimes, leaders refuse to plan or to revise plans simply because they are resistant to change. Business Is ART is built on the premise of change. From changing how you do things simply by using the framework itself, to revising things along the way.

There are many theories and suggestions for dealing with resistance to change, and you can spend a great deal of time researching and implementing the many methodologies. But here is a good list of ten reasons people resist change. This list by Rosabeth Moss Kanter appeared in the *Harvard Business Review*.[2] In the following list, I've quoted the reason from the article and then described how each reason manifested itself in the $50 million example used throughout this book.

1. "Loss of control. Change interferes with autonomy and can make people feel that they've lost control over their territory." This was especially true in each of the four business sectors that existed in the company when I took over. Each team was its own island, only crossing paths with others at any company-sponsored events. With a few exceptions, most people got over this when they understood that they had something to gain as well as give.

2. "Excess uncertainty. If change feels like walking off a cliff blindfolded, then people will reject it." On the day my predecessor, Tom, stepped down from his role and I was introduced as his replacement, people cried. They genuinely loved this man. One of his great attributes was that he was very personable and had a great sense of humor. So, when it was time for me to be introduced as their new leader, I'd prepared a slide presentation that provided some real

information, but had more entertainment value than anything. For example, people knew that I would approach things differently than Tom, so I had a lead-in slide that asked, "What will Jon be doing?" On the next slide was a picture of me, in Tom's office, staring intently out the window. The caption read, "Just sittin' around…thinkin' about stuff." This put everyone immediately at ease, and while they never lost their love for Tom, they came to respect my leadership in its own right and were therefore willing to go in whatever direction I asked of them.

3. "Surprise, surprise! Decisions imposed on people suddenly, with no time to get used to the idea or prepare for the consequences, are generally resisted." There are two things for which I take direct credit in our success, and only two. One is that I surrounded myself with smart people: people who knew the business better than I. Two, I didn't "screw things up." That was actually my initial objective going in. The company had been acquired because the due diligence showed it had value, so the last thing I wanted to do as its new leader was destroy that value. One of the ways we preserved the business's value and formed the base for additional value is that I took my time. Believe me, I wanted to move much more quickly. But with proper advice and coaching, I took less of a gunslinger approach, shooting everything in my way, and more of an orchestra-conductor approach, leading the various parts of the company to work in harmony at the tempo I prescribed. I was clearly in charge, but part of the team. If it was a turnaround

situation, the gunslinger approach might have been more necessary because time would have been of the essence.

4. "Everything seems different. Change is meant to bring something different, but how different?" As previously mentioned, not everyone got on board with the changes we were introducing with our growth plans, but the people who didn't believe in our growth plan left of their own accord or by invitation fairly early on in the process. The rest accepted the change either because they felt they had no choice or because they felt they in some way were carrying out the change. Both of these assertions were true, but they were enabled by communication. We purposely invited the staff to participate. We engaged many influencers in the vision and planning process. We formally communicated with the entire staff and we regularly reported progress and celebrated success. In this kind of environment, "different" is good.

5. "Loss of face. By definition, change is a departure from the past." There certainly were many leaders and staff at the company, perhaps the majority, who felt a strong association with the past and a great deal of pride in it. From the start, I made it clear that they should indeed be proud of their past and that, after all, they had been acquired specifically because they had done such good work. So we celebrated the past. But a couple of years later, I felt there was still too much nostalgia getting in our way. Around that time, I read a book entitled *The CEO and the Monk* by Robert Catell, Kenny Moore, and Glenn Rifkin, in which

the principal author, Catell, describes a time when his company literally held a funeral for the old company so that people could get over the nostalgia and get on with accepting change. As corny as it sounded, we decided to do the same. And so, during one of our quarterly all-employee meetings, we held a memorial service for the old company (using the name it had before acquisition). During the service, we invited people to come up and say a few words. Over the preceding weeks, I had collected input from random employees and included their thoughts in the eulogy. These ranged from serious to ridiculous, but they all had meaning to the employees. For example, it had been three years since they had been given a Christmas turkey by the previous owners. It was something that was gone forever, and they missed it. So we acknowledged it in the eulogy and let it go. The service seemed to have a truly positive effect, and I would do it again in a similar situation.

6. "Concerns about competence. Can I do it? Confidence, or lack thereof, can be a killer." One of the greatest aids to fighting this was the coach I hired shortly after being assigned to lead the company. He helped me with confidence in two ways. First, he helped me to gain and keep confidence by providing me with an unbiased, confidential ear. He was a neutral party who I could bounce ideas off and who provided me with a framework on which to build my own vision and strategy. Much of what he taught me is included in Business Is ART. But he also helped me understand how to build confidence in my leadership team, and

ultimately, among our employee base. Once they got over the initial shock of hearing that we had set an objective to grow to a $50 million business, the vast majority of the team never felt we couldn't do it. They believed.

7. "More work. Here is a universal challenge. Change is indeed more work." When I was first assigned to run the company, it was pretty normal to look out at the parking lot at 4:30 p.m. and see only a couple of cars, one of them mine. It was very much an eight-hour-day culture. This may have been the toughest challenge of all because the type of change we were introducing was going to be pretty massive and would require a lot of work. As mentioned, we desperately wanted to keep the fun culture that existed, but there was no way we would achieve our goals by continuing to operate the way we always had. Before our own subsequent acquisition, the point at which we lost control, we had all kinds of purposeful methods for addressing bigger workloads. We offered incentives, we delegated, we hired temporary assistance when needed, and we staffed up according to plans, sometimes betting that the revenue-generating income would follow instead of waiting for the additional work and then scrambling to hire qualified staff. For a while, it was no big deal to see cars in the parking lot well past the former quitting hour because people wanted to be there. We also focused on ways to let people do things after hours at home, after they spent some quality time with the family and took care of their own personal business. After acquisition, it was

standard to see a full parking lot well after normal hours because we were being squeezed so hard that no one could complete their work in the course of a "normal" work day. Not surprisingly, employee satisfaction and engagement fell off. When they *want* to be there putting in extra time, you as a leader have done your job. When they continuously *have* to be there putting in extra time, you have problems.

8. "Ripple effects. Like tossing a pebble into a pond, change creates ripples, reaching distant spots in ever-widening circles." One disruptive ripple effect I encountered in our march to $50 million was technical in nature. The company had been operating in traditional "mom and pop" fashion, but we were graduating to a point well beyond that. At one point, we released a major system modification to accommodate a brand-new client that brought substantial growth to our business. But we did it without a stress test to see what it would do to our existing, loyal customers, which was, as it turns out, to bring the system to its knees for several hours. This happened while we were wining and dining clients at an annual industry conference. After far too many cocktails, one of these clients, whose system had been down all day long, proceeded to let me know in some very unflattering terms just what he thought of me, and it wasn't anything good. He also offered to punch me in the mouth, à la Mike Tyson, if that should be my desire. I declined. Somehow, I managed to keep my cool, but I was literally up all night with this guy, listening to him rant and rave about what a terrible person

and leader I was. The next day, I let his employer know that while I was deeply sorry for the harm we had caused their business the previous day, I would not tolerate that kind of treatment. Together, we got through it, but needless to say, this incident revealed a large hole in our internal processes and highlighted the ripple effect our growth could have on everyone with a stake in it.

9. "Past resentments. The ghosts of the past are always lying in wait to haunt us." To some extent, the funeral we held for the old company took care of some resentments, but it probably dealt more directly with current resentment about not doing things as they had been done in the past. Otherwise, to my recollection, one of the more challenging things to get over was not so much a single point of resentment, but rather a habit of feeling like a mistake could not be admitted to, and if it was, the admission was accompanied with an overpowering urge to point fingers. We fought this by continually creating an environment in which mistakes were OK, as long as we learned from them, fixed them, and eliminated or reduced the risk of repeating them. But just as importantly, we insisted on an environment in which we didn't point fingers, we looked for solutions. While I was in control, no one ever lost their job because they made a mistake. Repeatedly making the same mistake, yes. Making it once, learning from it, and moving on, no. This helped to reduce the potential for resentment.

10. "Sometimes the threat is real. Now we get to true pain and politics. Change is resisted because it can hurt."

This was certainly true in our case. Tom's departure itself was very emotional. There were some people, some roles, and even some facilities that were there simply because of tradition. There were some "sacred cows." When we reorganized and subsequently laid off a dozen or so people who hadn't necessarily done anything wrong, but just didn't fit the new model, it was hard, but we did it as gently as possible. My human resources director, Michelle, was incredible. I once told her, "When it's my turn to be let go, I want you to do it." She had a way of making people feel good about themselves and helping them feel as good as they could feel about losing their job. The first time we let several people go, we made an announcement that anyone who wanted to could join me and some others in the lobby to have a moment of silence or say a prayer for those who were leaving. Almost the entire employee base showed up. We had trouble fitting everyone in, but we did it. Even though it was a horrible feeling for all involved, we humanized our actions as much as we could.

■ THE CHAPTER 9 WRAP

In this chapter, you learned more about the hypnopompic state than you ever dreamed possible (pun intended). We also discussed the importance of turning raw data into information and why visual representations of that information help us interpret it.

We introduced the Ping Chart as an additional tool for your arsenal that is different from the standard graphs and charts you may be accustomed to. Its intent is to help you visualize the health of your business by visualizing the health of the KPIs that you have defined as important.

Although the foundation of the Ping Chart is fairly complex, its use is pretty simple: determine the coordinates and plot the "ping" on the chart, adding a splash of color. The color is not just for visual appeal. It too conveys a message about whether things are going pretty well, just passably, or not well at all.

The Ping Chart can be used to study correlation or cause and effect between pairs of KPIs, or to track single KPIs. Up to four pairs or individual KPIs can be displayed on one Ping Chart: one pair or individual KPI per quadrant.

Once the information is visualized, there are two important things to do: interpret the information and determine what actions you will take based on this interpretation. This is step twelve of the twelve-step approach to business as ART: continually review, assess, refine, and modify the previous steps as necessary.

Do it, even if you don't want to. Like diet and exercise, it's for your own good and longevity, even though eating pizza on the couch while watching Mike Tyson get punched in the mouth may sound more entertaining.

Finally, we discussed Rosabeth Moss Kanter's list of ten reasons people resist change. I've added some real-life examples of how these reasons manifested themselves in our quest to turn our company into a $50 million business, and how we dealt with those manifestations.

The next chapter is a summary of everything discussed in the previous chapters.

Please answer the following questions before proceeding:

1. What tools do you use to track KPIs?
2. How do you document and link your KPIs to your business plan and to your strategic plan?
3. To use an online tool that does this for you, and helps you easily move through the twelve-step Business Is ART process, please go to www.businessisart.net to subscribe.

TEN

THE BUSINESS
IS ART WRAP

Like many artists, I have struggled with the notion
of art as a business. It doesn't come naturally
to me but it is a very important part of being
an artist. I don't intend to be a factory but I do
plan to become wiser in the areas of business.
DION ARCHIBALD, CONTEMPORARY
AUSTRALIAN PAINTER

Andy Warhol said that good business is the best kind of art, and this is a great way to look at it. Too many times, business is presented as a science, scaring artists, be they painters, roofers, bakers, or plumbers, away from learning and exercising good business practices. Too many times, the notion of business as a science makes business leaders think that science, processes, methodology, and practices rule the day, forgetting the artful aspects of business.

Business is both an art and a science, and the most successful business leaders wear both hats (or aprons) equally. Chances are good that only one comes naturally, so learning the other becomes a discipline. Many avoid that discipline because approaches, methodologies, and templates seem too difficult and more complex than they need to get into. So much of business philosophy and theory is geared toward the large business, so much that owners of small businesses don't have the time or resources to follow such substantial methods.

The purpose of this book and the Business Is ART framework is to provide the small and medium-sized business owner or organizational leader with a simplified approach to *articulating* the vision, strategy, business plan, and key performance indicators, metrics, or objectives by which success is measured; *revising* those plans along the way; and *tracking* progress to better understand the actions required to go back and do it all over again, in a continuous cycle.

The world is not a static place, so you have to change with it.

This book and its accompanying software identifies a twelve-step process for treating business as ART and provides you with templates, examples, and real-life stories to help you create your own masterpiece.

The twelve steps are as follows:

1. Briefly articulate the vision.
2. Conduct a self-assessment that includes your own personal definition of success.
3. Paint the picture by creating a document of at most three pages, or better yet, an actual work of art such

as a painting, a video, or a web site that visually tells your story.

4. Revise or refine the vision if necessary.
5. Honestly assess today's reality versus tomorrow's vision.
6. Recognize the gaps between the vision and today's reality.
7. Identify goals that you will have to meet in order to close the gap, and define objectives that will measure the rate of success in achieving those goals.
8. Identify specific initiatives, projects, or actions that have to be taken to realize those objectives.
9. Determine how you will manage the initiatives (project planning) and measure progress toward the completion of those initiatives.
10. Determine how you will manage the business itself.
11. Execute the plans and regularly measure your progress.
12. Continue to review, assess, refine, and modify the previous steps as necessary.

Chapter 1 walked through steps one through three in more detail and provided some real-life examples of how they were applied to an objective I had of turning a $21 million company that I had been hired to run into a $50 million business. It all started with a vision.

In that chapter, I discuss the concept of the painted picture described in Cameron Herold's book *Double Double*. A key difference between the vision and the painted picture is that the vision is a brief statement, whereas the painted picture provides more detail. Neither focuses on how to get there. Instead, they focus on what the desired end state is.

I provide some examples of questions to ask to paint your picture. Imagine that you have just traveled three years into the future and are walking around at your place of business, making observations and answering those questions.

I suggest creating a literal work of art to paint the picture, be it something that hangs on the wall, a website, a video, a song, or anything else that tells any stakeholder exactly what you envision in a brief moment. It is important that others understand your painted picture so that they are likely to get on board to help you realize your vision.

Chapter 2 provides a little advice to consider before and while completing steps one through three. In this chapter, we stepped away from process (science) for a bit and focused on the art of freestyle dancing. We discussed how some people throw off the shackles of choreography and in so doing, sometimes create a brand-new dance step. But often in business, we are reapplying or reinventing an old move created long, long ago.

Throwing off the shackles of choreography is necessary in order to stay relevant, but a willingness and desire to do so is not enough. You also must have a plan for how to proceed once the shackles have been removed. It does no good to throw off the shackles, only to stand there and wait for someone to slap them back on.

Sometimes it takes a willingness to explore to figure out how to throw off the shackles of choreography. You have to try applying old solutions to new problems. You have to try applying new solutions to new problems. And you have to try applying new solutions to old problems. But the important thing is to try and to take calculated risks.

In chapter 3, we returned to the twelve-step approach, addressing steps four through eight, which principally are sections of the strategic plan, and we identified some myths about strategic planning.

We also discussed and gave examples for steps four through eight of the twelve-step approach to business as ART and went into some detail about the difference between strategic plans and strategic initiatives.

This chapter introduced the notion of a ProCESS Strategy: a strategic plan that focuses on four cornerstones:

1. **Pro**fitability
2. **C**ustomer satisfaction
3. **E**mployee **s**atisfaction
4. **S**ocial responsibility

Finally, we discussed the elements of a one-page strategic plan template to help you quickly, efficiently organize your thoughts and document a strategy.

In chapter 4, we discussed the difference between strategic planning and strategic management, and we discussed steps nine through twelve of the twelve-step process in more detail.

In this chapter, we briefly defined strategic management as the management of today's tasks with an eye on tomorrow's vision. A key to successful strategic management is to determine *how* you will manage. The best and most popular project management methodologies are based on the Project Management Institute's Project Management Body of Knowledge (PMBOK). But attempting to apply all that PMBOK has to offer is usually overkill and can put you into a cycle of completing process for process's sake.

We summarize the basic elements of a solid project plan and go through the success factors critical to strategic management, including your willingness to delegate to others and how you strategically manage clients.

This led us to chapter 5 and the subject of behavior management. The first step in establishing a behavior management strategy is to identify the behavior that will achieve the results you want. Along the way, monitor whether or not the behavior management tools you have put in place are creating the results you want.

In this chapter, we identified and discussed the three pillars of behavior management: desire, emotion, and knowledge, and the importance of each one to your behavior management strategy.

We also discussed five common myths about behavior management, including the myth that a behavior management strategy necessarily costs money. We discussed how tools like bonus and P4P plans can and should positively contribute to the top and bottom line, resulting in a net cost of zero and a net gain of something greater than zero.

Be careful to design bonus and P4P plans that encourage the right behaviors. Poorly designed plans can have the exact opposite effect to what was intended. Remember that no one thing will motivate and inspire the desired behavior in everyone, so your strategy should include multiple tools and techniques.

Regardless of how you approach behavior management, it starts at the top. It starts with you.

In chapter 6, we discussed the difference between a strategic plan and a business plan. This chapter introduces a simplified, table-driven template that helps you produce a minimal business plan. It also provides a one-page executive summary that you should complete after filling in the details of the business plan, or that you can use as a watered-down business plan.

Finally, we discussed how a business plan can help you make decisions, sometimes tough ones, that might be more difficult to identify or make in the absence of a plan.

In chapter 7 we discussed the importance of key performance indicators (KPIs) or performance metrics. The chapter provided you with a list of KPIs to consider, and categorized them by "perspectives." Don't identify too many metrics, though; find the metrics that have the most meaning to you.

In this chapter, we also provided you with the real-life example of how we determined KPIs on our $50 million quest by working backward from client and industry requirements and from our vision. Start with the end in mind.

In chapter 8, we discussed pairing metrics to track correlation and cause and effect. Here, we defined the word "correlation" and discussed how it is different from cause and effect.

When KPIs are observed on their own, they don't tell the whole tale, and you may be missing the point. A better way to look at KPIs is by pairing them with other KPIs where there is a correlation or a cause and effect that is of interest to you. Finally, this chapter provides you with an extensive list of possible KPIs and recommended pairings of each.

In chapter 9, we discussed the importance of turning raw data into information and why visual representations of that information help us interpret it. We introduced the Ping Chart as an additional tool that is different from the standard graphs and charts you may be accustomed to. The Ping Chart can be used to study correlation or cause and effect between pairs of KPIs, or to track single KPIs.

Once the information is visualized, there are two important things to do: interpret the information and determine what actions you will take based on this interpretation. This is step twelve of the twelve-step approach to business as ART: continually review, assess, refine, and modify the previous steps as necessary.

Finally, we explored why people resist change, with some real-life examples of how these reasons manifested themselves in our quest to turn our company into a $50 million business.

■ THE BUSINESS IS ART SOFTWARE

With the purchase of this book, you are entitled to a three-month trial of the Business Is ART software. It is a cloud-based application, meaning all you need to use it is a web browser. It is based on the principles, processes, and templates of Business Is ART, and you can use it to apply everything you have learned from this and other sources.

Its objective is to provide you, the small to medium-sized business owner or organizational leader, with an easy-to-follow method for Articulating, Revising, and Tracking your business, from the vision through the strategy and the business plan to the KPIs, and pairing thereof, that are important to you.

Ultimately, its purpose is to provide you with a tool to help you visually, literally picture success.

For access to this tool, go to www.businessisart.net and subscribe.

■ A FINAL WORD

In July 2011, at age twenty-seven, my dear nephew Nathan took his own life in his Denver apartment. His death affected all of his friends and family, particularly his mother—my sister—in our own unique ways.

For me, it was a wake-up call to make some significant changes in my own life. Most notably, I realized it was time for me to stop focusing on my own success and start focusing on the success of others. To do so, I had to make and carry out many life-changing decisions. I had to help myself first before I could help others.

But when I was ready, and because of my educational and professional background in business, it made the most sense to me that business and executive consulting was one place where I could help others. This was an opportunity to share my education, experience, and lessons learned with others so that they could be more successful. If nothing else, a consultant provides a safe and confidential environment for clients to talk to someone who "gets" what they are going through. It was through this decision to consult that Business is ART was born, with the express purpose of helping others to improve their odds of success.

During my time leading the company I've used repeatedly as an example in this book, I had the help and support of so many people. They started out as business acquaintances, and most ended up as lifelong friends. At no time during my tenure as their leader (or client) did I feel alone or without access to answers, and that made all the difference in the world.

Leadership can be isolating. If this book and the Business Is ART framework provide just one person with some of the tools they need to feel less overwhelmed, then it will have been well worth the time and expense to write it.

Thank you so much for reading. I hope you found it both informative and entertaining. But most importantly, I hope you found it useful and that you will follow up and actually do something with the things you have learned or picked up on through this book.

And *that*, my friends, is a wrap!

INDEX

Abbott, Scott, 235
accounting objectives, in
    business plan, 162
account manager, for customers,
    93–94, 97–98
accounts receivable, and KPIs
    pairings, 229–31, 233
Albright, S. Christian, 195
"all-in" moment, 27–28
Angelou, Maya, 106
Archibald, Dion, 248
art
    as business, 5–6, 248–49
    business as, 1–3
    business is (*See* Business Is
      ART)
    of painted picture, 24, 28
    and radical change, 41–42,
      49–50
ART (articulate, revise, track),
    1–2, 19.
    See also Business Is ART

articulate, in ART, 2, 129, 167, 249
assumptions, in business plan,
    162–63

backward work, in plans, 45–46
Ballard, Robert, 51
Behavior Breakthrough, The
    (Jacobs), 101–2, 103, 112, 131
behavior management
    bonus plans, 120–25, 130–37
    and common courtesy, 106–10
    description and goal, 102–3,
      140, 253–54
    and desire, 110–11, 112–13
    and emotion, 110–11, 113–19
    expectations, 125–31
    as expense, 123–25
    importance, 101–2
    incentives, 121–23, 125–26, 130
    and knowledge, 110–11, 119–20
    leader's role, 103–6, 127–29,
      131

myths, 120–31
pay-for-performance plans,
131–32, 137–39
pillars of, 110–20
strategy development, 111–12
tools, 106
Bethune, Gordon, 212
big-box stores, 35–38
BlackBerry, 50
bonus plans
and behavior management,
120–25, 130–37
in business plan, 159–60
definition, 132
as expense, 123–25
objectives in, 133–36, 159
boundaries. *See* shackles
brainstorming, for plans, 44–45
budget, in business plan, 148
business, as science and art, 1–3,
5–6, 248–49
Business Is ART
artist and scientist in lockstep,
5–6
and business plan, 167
and change, 237–38
concept and overview, 1–3, 5–6
and pairings, 198–99
purpose, 249
software, 255–56
steps, 6–8
and vision, 6–7, 8–10, 20,
66–72, 249
visualization (*See* Ping Chart
and Ping Charting)
See also twelve-step process of
Business Is ART
business plan
Business Is ART, 167
for decision-making, 165–75

description and role, 142–43,
254
execution and review, 165–67
importance, 143–44
learning through mistakes
and failures, 167–69
letting go of people, 169–75
one-page summary, 145
one-year objectives, 146–47
templates, 144–65

cash on hand, and KPIS pairing,
229–31, 233
Catell, Robert, 240–41
cause and effect, in metrics and
KPIS, 195–97, 206
change
and Business Is ART, 237–38
resistance to and acceptance
of, 237–45
and shackles, 39–41, 48–49
and success, 239–40
and workloads, 242–43
See also radical change
clients. *See* customers
colors and coloring, in Ping
Charting, 226–28, 231
commissions for sales, 124–25
common courtesy, 106–10
communication plan, 89
completion date, strategic plans,
62–64
complexity and complications,
simplification of, 219–20, 223
conclusion, in business plan, 145,
166
conferences, sponsorship, 98
confidence, 241–42
consulting, and needs of clients,
111

coordination, 194. *See also* pairing theory and metrics

corporate responsibility KPIS, 182, 186, 204

correlation, 193–95, 198

Cowell, Simon, 179

creativity, and hypnopompic state, 222–23

culture, and conformity, 40–41

current facilities, in business plan, 154–55

customer KPIS
list and definitions, 182, 184
pairings, 203, 207, 209–12, 229–31, 234

customer retention, 209–12

customers
firing of, 174–75
information and newsletters, 94–95
insincerity to, 96–99
strategic management, 93–96

customer satisfaction, 75, 96–97, 183, 209–10

data. *See* information

delegating, 90–92

Deming, W. Edwards, 207

desire, in behavior management, 110–11, 112–13

Double Double (Herold), 23–24, 33, 45

dreams, and creativity, 222–23

dress code, 40–41

Edison, Thomas, 5, 165

Eisenhower, Dwight D., 54

emotion
and behavior management, 110–11, 113–19

definition, 114
and mood, 114–15
of others, 115–19

employee KPIS
list and definitions, 182, 186
pairings, 204, 208, 211, 215–16

employees
behavior management (*See* behavior management)
churn rate, 211
emotions, 116–19
engagement, 215
expectations of employers, 125–30
incentives, 121–23, 125–26, 130
involvement, 27–28, 29–30
letting go of, 169–75
as resource, 35–36, 37
rewards for extra work, 89
satisfaction, 75, 183, 208, 215–16, 243
volunteer work and KPIS, 211–12, 214
workload and change, 242–43

employer, expectations of employees, 125–30. *See also* behavior management

"exception handle", 46

executive summary, in business plan, 145, 146–47

expenses, 123–25

exploration, and radical change, 50–52

failure, odds of, 143

failures and mistakes, learning from, 167–69, 244

fear and leaps of faith, 17–18, 39–41

finances, projections, 66–68

financial KPIS
    list and definitions, 182, 183–84
    pairings, 202–3, 205–9
financial plan, example, 145, 161–65
finger pointing, 167–68, 244
firing
    and behavior management,
        117, 125–29
    and business plan, 169–75
    and change, 245
    of customers, 174–75
fishbone diagrams, 197
4.0 grading scale, in Ping
    Charting, 223–24, 226–28,
    230–31
Frost, Bob, 179, 188
funeral, for old company, 241

Gerstner, Louis, Jr., 39–41
grading points, in Ping Chart,
    223–24, 226–28, 230–31
groupthink, avoidance, 44–45
growth rate and KPIS, 213, 229–31,
    232–34

Haney, Chris, 235
Harris, Guy, 140
Herold, Cameron, 23–24, 32, 45
hiring, 118–19, 126–29
Holtz, Lou, 180–81
Home Depot, 81
human resources. See employees
hypnopompic state, 222–23

IBM, change at, 39–41
ideas
    and shackles, 36–38, 40–41, 47
    and vision, 6
Ikea, 35–36, 37
images, importance, 220

impressionism, 41–42
incentive plans. See pay-for-
    performance plans
incentives, for employees, 121–23,
    125–26, 130
information
    and customers, 94
    interpretation and use,
        236–37
    and trivia, 235–36
    visualization (See Ping Chart
        and Ping Charting)
    See also metrics
infrastructure, in business plan,
    154–55
initiative vs. strategy, 63–64. See
    also strategic initiatives
innovation. See radical change
insincerity, 96–99
Ishikawa, Kaoru, 196–97

Jacobs, Steve, 101–2, 103, 112, 131
Jobs, Steve, 49

Kanter, Rosabeth Moss, 238
Kenny, Graham, 32
key performance indicators (KPIS)
    description, 3
    guidelines for use, 198, 200, 216
    importance and categories,
        181–83
    list and definitions in, 183–86
    pairing recommendations,
        200–216
    and pairing theory, 197–200
    and Ping Charting, 226, 228–34
    selection for KPIS tracking,
        187–90
    visualization (See Ping Chart
        and Ping Charting)

Key Performance Indicators (Marr), 182–83
knowledge, in behavior management, 110–11, 119–20
KPIS (key performance indicators). *See* key performance indicators (KPIS)

Landry, Tom, 103
leaders
     behavior management role, 103–6, 127–29, 131
     delegation, 90–92
leadership legacy statements, 19–23
leaps of faith, 17–18
learning by doing, 91–92
locations, in business plan, 154–55
loss. *See* profit and loss

Mandela, Nelson, 17
market analysis, 149
marketing and sales, 149–50, 151
     KPIS, 182, 184–85, 203, 212–14
marketing plan and product sales, in business plan, 145, 148–52
market share, and KPIS, 210–11, 212–14, 229–31, 233–34
Marr, Bernard, 182–83
methodologies
     in production, 153–54
     project management, 84–86
     and shackles, 86–87
     strategic management, 57, 252–53
     strategic plans and planning, 57
metrics
     cause and effect, 195–97, 206
     correlation, 193–95

definition, 3
honesty in, 178–79
importance, 177–80
one-year objectives, 146–47
and pairing theory (*See* pairing theory and metrics)
self-assessment, 14–17
tracking of performance, 180–82
visualization (*See* Ping Chart and Ping Charting)
See also key performance indicators (KPIS)
mission, personal, 11–12
mission statement, 31–32
mistakes and failures, learning from, 167–69, 244
mitigation, in business plan, 162–63
monetary rewards, 120–25
mood, and emotion, 114–15
Moore, Kenny, 240–41
music, and radical change, 41–42, 49–50

net profit, and KPIS pairing, 205–9, 229–31
newsletters, 94–95, 107
nonmonetary "awards", 123

objectives
     achievement and measure, 16
     identification, 70–71
     thinking big about, 190–91.
     See also metrics
old company, funeral for, 241
old ideas, and shackles, 36–38, 40–41, 47
Oliver, Garrett, 198–99
one-page plan, 73, 76–77

one-year objectives, 146–47
operating objectives, 156
operating plan, 145, 153–56
operational KPIS
  list and definitions, 182, 185–86
  pairings, 203–4, 214–15
  See also key performance
    indicators (KPIS)
organizational structure, in
  business plan, 153
overcomplication, simplification
  of, 219–20, 223

P3s (public–private partnerships),
  25
P4Ps (pay-for-performance plans),
  131–32, 137–39, 159–60
paint the picture
  in Business Is ART, 7, 23–25,
    249–51
  and vision, 23, 25–28
  visual aid, 24, 28, 33
pairing theory and metrics
  and Business Is ART, 198–99
  and correlation, 198
  description and overview,
    197–200, 254–55
  example, 201–5
  and food, 198–99
  KPIS recommendations,
    200–216
  metrics and KPIS, 197–200
  and Ping Charting, 226, 228–34
pay-for-performance plans (P4Ps),
  131–32, 137–39, 159–60
Penney, James Cash, 209
performance and metrics. *See*
  key performance indicators
    (KPIS); metrics
pictures, importance, 220

Ping Chart and Ping Charting
  colors and coloring, 226–28,
    231
  description, 3, 255
  foundations, 223–27
  4.0 grading scale and points,
    223–24, 226–28, 230–31
  interpretation, 232–34
  KPIS pairing, 226, 228–34
  origins, 222–23
  plotting, 227–32
  and sonar, 223, 224–26, 231
  steps, 232
pipeline opportunities, 67–68
planned facilities, in business
  plan, 155
plans and planning
  in Business Is ART, 249
  categories in, 13–14
  change and revision of, 237–38
  information in, 236–37
  for personal success, 13–15
  and shackles, 43–46
  three-year and four-year, 30–31
PMP certification, 85
ProCESS strategy, 75–76, 77, 183,
  252
production methodology, 153–54
product sales and marketing
  plan, 145, 148–52
products and services, in
  business plan, 148–52
profitability, in ProCESS, 75, 183
profit and loss, 163–64, 205–6,
  229–31, 232–33. *See also* revenue
Project Management Body of
  Knowledge (PMBOK), 84–86,
  253
project management
  methodologies, 84–86

project management
    professionals (PMPs), 85
project plan, components, 87–90,
    100
projects
    methodologies, 84–86, 87
    plan components, 87–90
    in strategic initiatives, 84–87
public–private partnerships
    (P3s), 25
purpose statement, 31–32, 115

quality, and KPIs, 214–15

radical change, 41–42, 49–52. *See
    also* change
recognition programs, 123
referrals, from customers, 96–97
resignations, 171–72
resources, assignment, 88
retention plans, 160–61
revenue
    growth rate and KPIs, 213,
        229–31, 232–34
    projections, 66–68
reverse engineering, for plans,
    45–46
revise, in ART, 2, 167, 236–38, 249
rewards, and behavior manage-
    ment, 120–22, 123, 130–31
reward structure, 89
Rifkin, Glenn, 240–41
risks, 88–89, 162–63
rumors, effects, 105–6
Rumsfeld, Donald, 90

sales and marketing, 149–50, 151
    KPIs, 182, 184–85, 203, 212–14
sales commissions, 124–25
sales forecast, 152

satisfaction
    of customers, 75, 96–97, 183,
        209–10
    of employees, 75, 183, 208,
        215–16, 243
schedule, 87–88
science of business, 1, 5–6,
    248–49
self-assessment
    in Business Is ART, 11–13
    categories in, 13–14
    and leadership legacy
        statements, 19–23
    metrics and template, 14–17
self-discovery and leaps of faith,
    16–18
service level agreements (SLAs),
    and KPIs, 188–89
services and products, in
    business plan, 148–52
shackles
    and big-box stores, 35–38
    and change, 39–41, 48–49
    concept, 35–36, 251–52
    in methodology, 86–87
    and old ideas, 36–38, 40–41, 47
    and radical change, 41–42,
        49–50
    removal strategies, 42–46
    and speed of development,
        46–47
    and staying relevant, 47–50
short-term gains, 55–56, 98
simplification, 219–20, 223
sincerity, 96–99
Six Sigma, and KPIs, 208
Snapchat, 46–47
social responsibility, 75–76,
    160–61, 183
    KPIs, 182, 186, 204, 208–9

software, for Business Is ART, 255–56

sonar, and Ping Charting, 223, 224–26, 231

Spiegel, Evan, 46

sponsorship, conferences and trade shows, 98

staffing and staffing plan, 145, 157–61

Stanford marshmallow experiment, 55–56

strategic initiatives
    definition and main points, 64–65, 71–72
    management, 84–87
    and PMBOK, 84–86, 253
    strategy vs., 64–65

strategic management
    and Business Is ART, 81–82, 83
    change of tactics, 83–84
    of customers, 93–96
    definition and description, 56, 80–81
    insincerity in, 96–99
    methodologies, 57, 252–53
    strategic planning vs., 81–82
    task management vs., 82–84

strategic plans and planning
    common elements, 73–75, 77
    completion date, 62–64
    definition, 55–56
    description and role, 54–55, 142
    execution and follow-up, 57–58
    methodologies, 57
    in the mind, 58–60
    myths and components, 60–66
    one-page plan, 73, 76–77
    size of, 61–62

strategic management vs., 81–82

time covered by, 60–61

strategy
    behavior management, 111–12
    change of, 83–84
    and daily survival, 84
    development, 30–31
    initiative vs., 63–64
    ProCESS strategy, 75–76, 77, 183, 252
    strategic initiatives vs., 64–65

strengths, improvement, 15–16

success
    and art, 19
    and business planning, 143–44
    celebration, 90
    and change, 239–40
    definition and achievement, 11–13
    fear and leaps of faith, 17–18
    odds of businesses, 143
    plan for, 13–15

sharing and teaching, 256–57

tactics. See strategy

targets. See metrics

task management, vs. strategic management, 82–84

templates
    business plan, 144–65
    one-page plan, 76–77
    self-assessment, 14–15
    See also worksheets

Titanic, 51

track, in ART, 2, 3, 19, 167, 249. See also information; metrics

trade shows, sponsorship, 98

training plan, in business plan, 158

trivia, and information, 235–36
Trivial Pursuit, 235–36
Turkey, John, 220
twelve-step process of Business
Is ART
in Business Is ART, 6–8,
249–50
in case study, 30–31
overview and purpose, 6–8,
249
painting the picture, 7, 23–25,
250–51
and self-assessment, 11–13
strategic management, 81–82,
83
vision in, 6–7, 8–10, 20, 66–72,
249

vision
assessment, 69–70
in Business Is ART, 6–7, 8–10,
20, 66–72, 249
development, 9–10, 26–28
gaps with reality, 70–71, 74
and painting the picture, 23,
25–28
personal, 11–12
realization, 28–30
revision and refinement,
66–68, 111
visualization, 23–25, 220–21. *See
also* Ping Chart and Ping
Charting
volunteer work and hours, and
KPIS, 211–12, 214

Watson, Thomas J., 40
"what if" questions, 50, 52
Who Says Elephants Can't Dance?
(Gerstner), 39–40

Wilber, Ken, 11
Winston, Wayne L., 195
working backwards, for plans,
45–46
work-life balance, 13
workloads, during change,
242–43
worksheets
accounting objectives, 162
assumptions, risks, and
mitigation, 161–62
bonus and incentive plan, 160
current and planned facilities,
155
market analysis, 149
one-year objectives and
performance, 147
operating objectives, 156
production methodology, 154
products and services, 148
profit and loss, 163–64
retention plans, 161
sales and marketing, 150–52
self-assessment, 14–15
staffing and recruiting, 157
training plan, 158
See also templates

X–Y grid and axis, and Ping
Charting, 223, 226–27

Zappe, Christopher, 195